초등학생의 영어 친구

리딩버디

READING BUDDY

3

리딩버디 3

지은이	NE능률 영어교육연구소
연구원	한정은, 강혜진, 이지연, 이윤주, 김은정
영문 교열	Lewis Hugh Hosie, Peter Morton, MyAn Le
디자인	장현정, 김연주
내지 일러스트	조희진, 양종은, 김동훈, 강난주, 진민지, 강윤주, 최영아
내지 사진	www.shutterstock.com, www.commons.wikimedia.org, www.flickr.com
맥편집	이정임
영업	한기영, 이경구, 박인규, 정철교, 김남준, 이우현
마케팅	박혜선, 남경진, 이지원, 김여진

42nd
Since 1980
Let's grow together
NE능률이
미래를
창조합니다.
건강한 배움의 고객가치를 제공하겠다는 꿈을 실현하기 위해
42년 동안 열심히 달려왔습니다.
앞으로도 끊임없는 연구와 노력을 통해
당연한 것을 멈추지 않고
고객, 기업, 직원 모두가 함께 성장하는 NE능률이 되겠습니다.
NE 능률

Dear Friends,

I'm your English Buddy!
Forget about all your worries.
I'm here to help you!
Let's smile! Let's learn! And let's have fun!

All the best,
Your English Buddy

★ HOW TO USE ★

재미있는 만화를 통해, 본문에서 배우게 될 내용과 문법을 확인해 보세요!

STORY

과학, 문화, 역사 등 다양한 주제에 대한 재미있고 정보성 가득한 이야기들이 수록되어 있습니다. 앞에서 배운 단어와 문법이 어떻게 쓰였는지 확인하며 독해 실력과 배경지식을 쌓아보세요!

Words to Learn

본격적으로 이야기를 읽기 전에 이야기에 나올 단어를 사진이나 그림과 함께 미리 학습해 보세요!

Grammar to Learn

해당 Unit에서 배울 핵심 문법을 그림과 예시 문장으로 제시했습니다. 독해 실력에 기본이 되는 문법 실력을 한층 더 업그레이드 해 보세요!

Word Check

앞서 배운 단어를 문제를 통해 확인해 볼 차례입니다. 그림 및 사진과 맞는 단어를 찾아보며 단어 실력을 점검해 보세요!

Grammar Check

간단한 문법 문제를 통해 이야기에 등장한 주요 문법을 제대로 학습했는지 점검해 보세요!

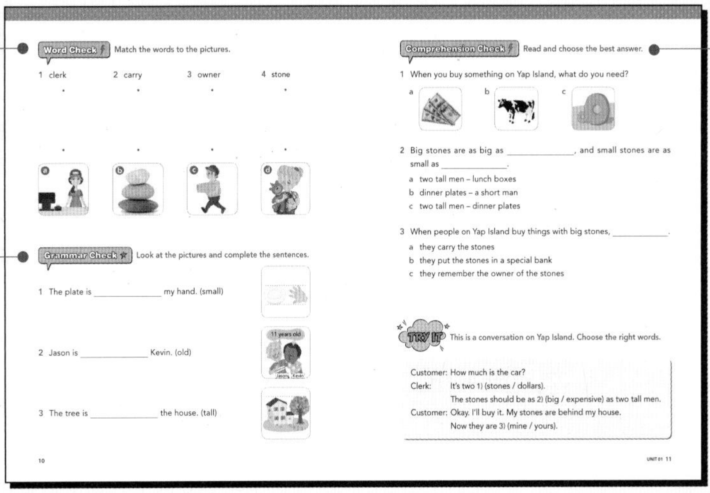

Word Check Match the words to the pictures.

1 clerk 2 carry 3 owner 4 stone

Grammar Check Look at the pictures and complete the sentences.

1 The plate is ____________ my hand. (small)

2 Jason is ____________ Kevin. (old)

3 The tree is ____________ the house. (tall)

Comprehension Check Read and choose the best answer.

1 When you buy something on Yap Island, what do you need?

a b c

2 Big stones are as big as ____________, and small stones are as small as ____________.

a two tall men – lunch boxes
b dinner plates – a short man
c two tall men – dinner plates

3 When people on Yap Island buy things with big stones, ____________.

a they carry the stones
b they put the stones in a special bank
c they remember the owner of the stones

TRY IT This is a conversation on Yap Island. Choose the right words.

Customer: How much is the car?
Clerk: It's two 1) (stones / dollars).
The stones should be as 2) (big / expensive) as two tall men.
Customer: Okay. I'll buy it. My stones are behind my house.
Now they are 3) (mine / yours).

10 UNIT 01 11

Comprehension Check

이야기를 잘 이해했는지 확인할 수 있는 문제들이 실려 있습니다. TRY IT 코너에서 조금 더 어려운 문제에도 도전하며 실력을 강화해 보세요!

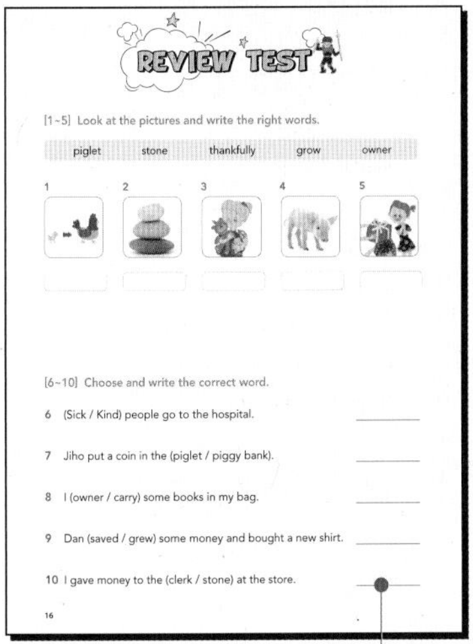

REVIEW TEST

[1~5] Look at the pictures and write the right words.

piglet stone thankfully grow owner

1 2 3 4 5

[6~10] Choose and write the correct word.

6 (Sick / Kind) people go to the hospital.

7 Jiho put a coin in the (piglet / piggy bank).

8 I (owner / carry) some books in my bag.

9 Dan (saved / grew) some money and bought a new shirt.

10 I gave money to the (clerk / stone) at the store.

16

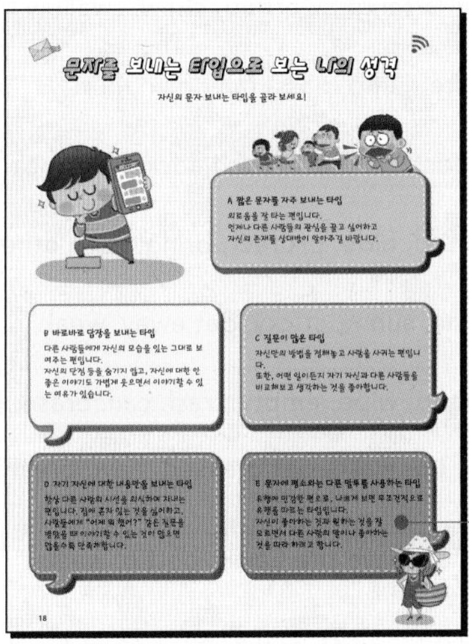

문자를 보내는 타입으로 보는 나의 성격

자신의 문자 보내는 타입을 골라 보세요!

18

재미있는 쉬어가기 코너를 통해 학습으로 지친 머리를 식혀보세요!

REVIEW TEST

각 Unit에서 학습한 단어와 문법, 그리고 이야기에 대한 이해도를 확인할 수 있는 다양한 문제가 실려 있습니다. 앞서 배운 내용을 다시 한번 확인해 보세요!

WORKBOOK

각 Unit에서 배운 단어와 문법을 여러 문제를 통해 확인하고 정리해 보세요.

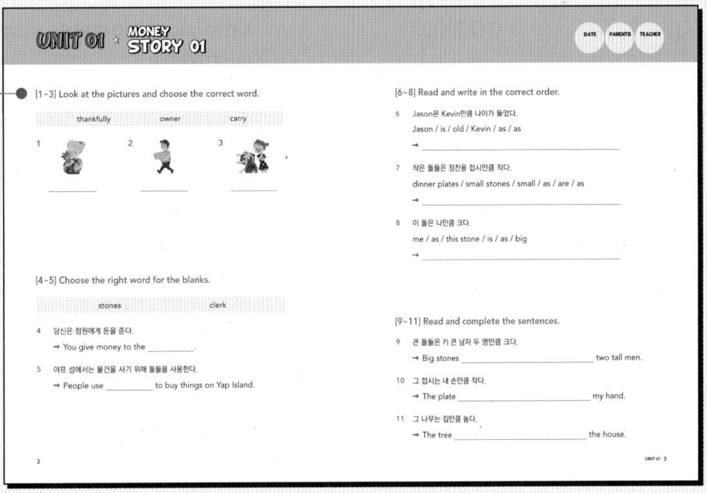

UNIT 01 MONEY STORY 01 DATE PARENTS TEACHER

[1~3] Look at the pictures and choose the correct word.

thankfully owner carry

1 2 3

[4~5] Choose the right word for the blanks.

stones clerk

4 당신은 점원에게 돈을 준다.
→ You give money to the ____________.

5 야프 섬에서는 물건을 사기 위해 돌들을 사용한다.
→ People use ____________ to buy things on Yap Island.

[6~8] Read and write in the correct order.

6 Jason은 Kevin만큼 나이가 들었다.
Jason / is / old / Kevin / as / as
→ ____________

7 작은 돌들은 정찬용 접시만큼 작다.
dinner plates / small stones / small / as / are / as
→ ____________

8 이 돌은 나만큼 크다.
me / as / this stone / is / as / big
→ ____________

[9~11] Read and complete the sentences.

9 큰 돌들은 키 큰 남자 두 명만큼 크다.
→ Big stones ____________ two tall men.

10 그 접시는 내 손만큼 작다.
→ The plate ____________ my hand.

11 그 나무는 집만큼 높다.
→ The tree ____________ the house.

2 UNIT 01 3

☆ OVERVIEW OF READING BUDDY ☆

	Unit	Title	Story	Key Words	Key Grammar
Level 1	01	INTERESTING PLACES	1	pilot, castle, wing, wall, museum	인칭대명사와 be동사
			2	vacation, hotel, have a meal, take a shower, feed, safe	명사의 복수형
	02	HEALTH	1	itchy, peanut, dangerous, see a doctor, take medicine	일반동사 현재형의 부정문
			2	gain weight, plate, taste, exercise, forget, hunger	명령문
	03	SPECIAL JOBS	1	perfect, lie down, leave, miss, chance	조동사 can
			2	pet, strange, worried, chew, swallow	be동사의 의문문
	04	HOBBIES	1	skate, jump, pass, fall down, hurt	일반동사의 3인칭 단수형
			2	collect, famous, touch, locked, unlock	want to-v
	05	NATURE	1	scared, hide, protect, bring, each other	형용사의 역할
			2	shine, sunny, sticky, get away, weak	조동사 can't
	06	SCHOOL LIFE	1	sweep, wipe, empty, trash can, erase, plant	It's time to-v
			2	get up, wash, get dressed, have breakfast, favorite	일반동사의 의문문
	07	SAVE THE EARTH	1	action, save the Earth, bottle, waste, recycle	청유문
			2	polar bear, the North Pole, spend, visit, tour, break	부정명령문
	08	FAIRY TALES	1	be lost, woods, cold, yummy, bread	There is/are
			2	magic, lamp, wish, comic book, cozy	Here is/are
Level 2	01	FOOD & COOKING	1	follow, recipe, cucumber, carrot, add	일반동사의 과거형
			2	astronaut, vegetable, hard, package, pour, microwave	의문사
	02	SPECIAL DAYS	1	the United States, celebrate, chocolate, interesting, each other	시간을 나타내는 전치사
			2	pick up, several, choose, athlete, rich	관사 the
	03	SUPERHEROES	1	prison, peace, delivery, fast, climb	조동사 will
			2	cape, resemble, attack, be afraid of, strong, train	등위접속사 and, but
	04	MY PET	1	apartment, bark, loudly, neighbor, allergic	셀 수 있는 명사와 셀 수 없는 명사
			2	grow, smart, smile, greet, guest	형용사의 순서

	Unit	Title	Story	Key Words	Key Grammar
	05	CULTURE	1	first, sour, second, beak, third	call+목적어+목적보어
			2	invite, dessert, tooth, hold, coin, tradition	What으로 시작하는 감탄문
	06	GOOD LUCK & BAD LUCK	1	symbol, around the world, wave, bill, wallet	장소를 나타내는 전치사
			2	mirror, broken, fence, sign, fail one's test	위치를 나타내는 전치사
	07	TRAVEL THE WORLD	1	travel, careful, rule, subway, flush the toilet, pay a fine	조동사 should
			2	be made of, worry, sleeping bag, fun, afternoon	go+v-ing
	08	HOW STRANGE!	1	win, try one's best, terrible, wear, playground, step	일반동사 과거형의 부정문
			2	stick, behavior, colorful, cover, start	how+형용사 ~?
Level 3	01	MONEY	1	clerk, stone, thankfully, carry, owner	원급 비교
			2	save, piggy bank, piglet, grow, sick	비교급
	02	ENVIRONMENT	1	climb, heavy, oxygen bottle, among, light, trash	최상급
			2	scientist, cow, hurt, fart, burp	감탄문
	03	MY OPINION	1	hallway, enter, behave, record, uncomfortable	감각동사+형용사
			2	learn, draw, outside, lake, nature, miss	빈도부사
	04	SHOPPING	1	cart, way, reason, full, push, secret	목적보어가 있는 동사
			2	look for, flavor, price, be made from, cheaply, fair	종속접속사 when, because, if
	05	GOOD INVENTIONS	1	normal, press, remote control, pick up, technology, convenient	감각동사+형용사 vs. 감각동사 like+명사
			2	across, invent, traffic light, side, copy	동명사 vs. to부정사
	06	TECHNOLOGY	1	sign, painting, rule, visitor, blind	조동사 may
			2	turn off, connect, machine, control, break down	현재진행형
	07	IN SPACE	1	astronaut, space, float, spaceship, tie	조동사 must, have to
			2	turn on, shoot, loud, silent, turn down	조동사 must와 cannot
	08	TRADITIONS	1	doll, worry, take away, pillow, disappear	tell+간접목적어+직접목적어
			2	hang from, cliff, hold onto, honey, hive, fall	동명사의 역할

★ CONTENTS ★

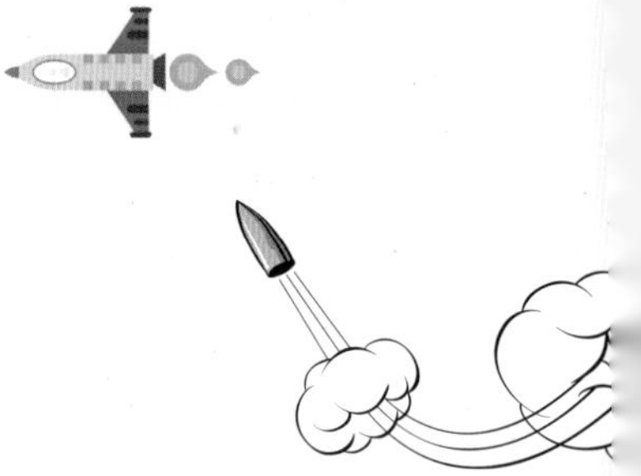

UNIT 01
MONEY
Read and guess the stories.
Can I buy your pig? Here is a stone.
No, it should be as big as my pig.
This piggy bank should be bigger than this stone.

STORY 01

Words to Learn Look at the pictures and read the words.

clerk

stone

thankfully

carry

owner

Grammar to Learn Look at the picture and read the sentences.

This stone is	**as big as**	me.
This stone is	**as small as**	my bag.

When you buy something, you ask "How much is it?"

Then you give the money to the **clerk**.

But on Yap Island, it is different.

People there use **stone**s to buy things.

Big stones are as big as two tall men.

Small stones are as small as dinner plates.

How do they move such big stones?

Thankfully, they don't **carry** them.

They just keep the stones somewhere and remember the **owner**.

> **배경지식**
> 야프 섬에서 가장 큰 부자는 가장 큰 돌을 배로 싣고 오다가 난파를 당하여 바닷속에 빠뜨린 사람이라고 합니다. 하지만 바닷속의 돌도 재산으로 인정되어 거래에 이용할 수 있다고 합니다.

MAIN IDEA ☆☆

The story is about ________________.

□ how to buy things on Yap Island

□ how to save money on Yap Island

Word Check

Match the words to the pictures.

1 clerk   2 carry   3 owner   4 stone

Grammar Check

Look at the pictures and complete the sentences.

1 The plate is ________________ my hand. (small)

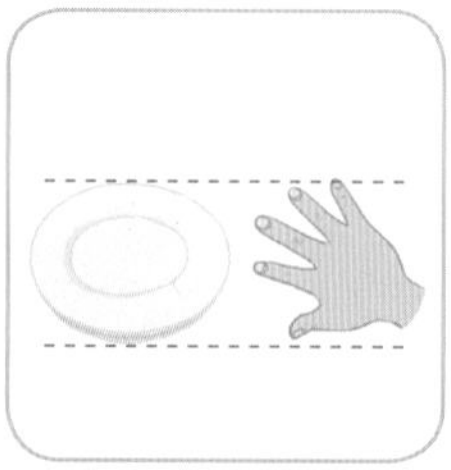

2 Jason is ________________ Kevin. (old)

3 The tree is ________________ the house. (tall)

Comprehension Check

Read and choose the best answer.

1 When you buy something on Yap Island, what do you need?

a 

b 

c 

2 Big stones are as big as ______________, and small stones are as small as ______________.

a two tall men – lunch boxes

b dinner plates – a short man

c two tall men – dinner plates

3 When people on Yap Island buy things with big stones, ______________.

a they carry the stones

b they put the stones in a special bank

c they remember the owner of the stones

TRY IT

This is a conversation on Yap Island. Choose the right words.

Customer: How much is the car?

Clerk: It's two 1) (stones / dollars).
The stones should be as 2) (big / expensive) as two tall men.

Customer: Okay. I'll buy it. My stones are behind my house.
Now they are 3) (mine / yours).

STORY 02

Words to Learn

Look at the pictures and read the words.

save

piggy bank

piglet

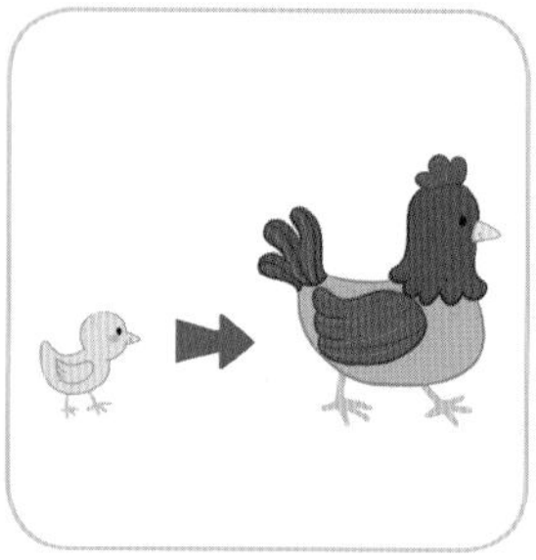
grow

sick

Grammar to Learn

Look at the picture and read the sentences.

The piglet is	bigger than	the kitten.
	older than	

tall	**taller**
large	**larger**
thin	**thinner**
easy	**easier**
difficult	**more difficult**
good	**better**

Why do people **save** money in **piggy banks**?

Here is the story.

There was a boy in a small town. His name was Wilbur.

One day, he bought a **piglet**.

It was much smaller than him.

But it **grew** and grew.

It became much bigger than him.

Wilbur sold it and saved the money to help **sick** people.

People wanted to be as kind as Wilbur.

They made piggy banks and saved money like he did.

MAIN IDEA ☆☆

The story is about ______________.

☐ the first pig

☐ the first piggy bank

Word Check Choose the right picture for each word.

1 piglet ______

2 grow ______

3 sick ______

4 save ______

a 

b 

c 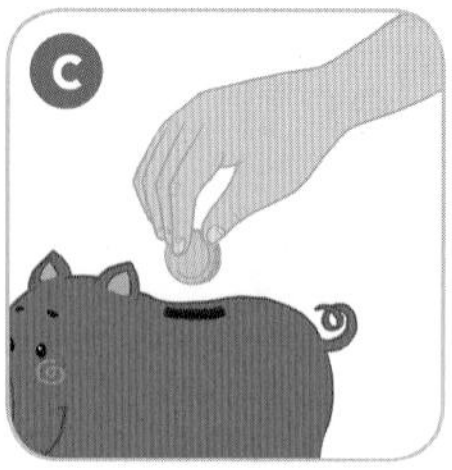

d 

Grammar Check Look at the pictures and complete the sentences.

1 The puppy is ______________ the chicken. (small)

2 Tom is ______________ Jake. (tall)

3 Science is ______________ English for me. (easy)

Comprehension Check

Read and choose the best answer.

1 Check True or False.

a Wilbur lived in a big city. True False

b Wilbur bought a piglet. True False

c The pig became bigger than Wilbur. True False

2 Wilbur sold his pig ________________.

a to buy a big house

b to help sick people

c to buy more piglets

3 People made piggy banks because ________________.

a they wanted to be as big as Wilbur

b they wanted to be as rich as Wilbur

c they wanted to be as kind as Wilbur

TRY IT

Number the sentences in the correct order.

1) ______ Wilbur helped sick people.

2) ______ Wilbur sold his pig and saved the money.

3) ______ Wilbur bought a piglet, and it grew and grew.

4) ______ People made piggy banks and saved money like Wilbur.

REVIEW TEST

[1~5] Look at the pictures and write the right words.

piglet　　stone　　thankfully　　grow　　owner

1

2

3

4

5

[6~10] Choose and write the correct word.

6 (Sick / Kind) people go to the hospital. ____________

7 Jiho put a coin in the (piglet / piggy bank). ____________

8 I (owner / carry) some books in my bag. ____________

9 Dan (saved / grew) some money and bought a new shirt. ____________

10 I gave money to the (clerk / stone) at the store. ____________

[11~12] Look at the pictures and complete the sentences.

11 Today is ________________ yesterday. (hot)

Yesterday	Today
30°C	33°C

12 Ally's hair is ________________ Lisa's hair. (long)

[13~14] Read and answer.

When you buy something, you ask "How much is it?"
Then you give the money to the clerk.
But on Yap Island, it is ___________.
People there use stones to buy things.
Big stones are as big as two tall men.
Small stones are as small as dinner plates.
How do they move such big stones?
Thankfully, they don't carry them.
They just keep the stones somewhere
and remember the owner.

13 Choose the word for the blank.

a same
b different
c dangerous

14 Check True or False about Yap Island.

a The size of the stones is always the same when they buy things. True False

b People always carry stones to buy things. True False

문자를 보내는 타입으로 보는 나의 성격

자신의 문자 보내는 타입을 골라 보세요!

A 짧은 문자를 자주 보내는 타입

외로움을 잘 타는 편입니다.
언제나 다른 사람들의 관심을 끌고 싶어하고
자신의 존재를 상대방이 알아주길 바랍니다.

B 바로바로 답장을 보내는 타입

다른 사람들에게 자신의 모습을 있는 그대로 보여주는 편입니다.
자신의 단점 등을 숨기지 않고, 자신에 대한 안 좋은 이야기도 가볍게 웃으면서 이야기할 수 있는 여유가 있습니다.

C 질문이 많은 타입

자신만의 방법을 정해놓고 사람을 사귀는 편입니다.
또한, 어떤 일이든지 자기 자신과 다른 사람들을 비교해보고 생각하는 것을 좋아합니다.

D 자기 자신에 대한 내용만을 보내는 타입

항상 다른 사람의 시선을 의식하며 지내는 편입니다. 집에 혼자 있는 것을 싫어하고, 사람들에게 "어제 뭐 했어?" 같은 질문을 받았을 때 이야기할 수 있는 것이 많으면 많을수록 만족해합니다.

E 문자에 평소와는 다른 말투를 사용하는 타입

유행에 민감한 편으로, 나쁘게 보면 무조건적으로 유행을 따르는 타입입니다.
자신이 좋아하는 것과 원하는 것을 잘 모르면서 다른 사람의 말이나 좋아하는 것을 따라 하려고 합니다.

UNIT 02
ENVIRONMENT
Read and guess the stories.
This is the highest mountain in the world.
How high it is!
How terrible the smell is!
It is the most terrible smell!

STORY 01

Words to Learn

Look at the pictures and read the words.

climb

heavy

oxygen bottle

among

light

trash

Grammar to Learn

Look at the picture and read the sentences.

Everest is	**the highest**	building of the three.
Halla is	**the lowest**	

old	old**est**
large	larg**est**
hot	hot**test**
heavy	heav**iest**
expensive	**most** expensive
good	**best**

Mt. Everest is the highest mountain in the world.

Many people try to **climb** it.

When they go up, climbers' bags are **heavy** with a lot of things — **oxygen bottle**s, tents, and other things.

Oxygen bottles are the heaviest things **among** them.

These heavy things make climbing harder.

So after the climbers use things, they leave them on Mt. Everest.

This makes their bags **light**er.

The mountain is still beautiful.

But there is so much **trash**!

MAIN IDEA ☆☆

The story is about ____________.

□ life on Mt. Everest

□ trash on Mt. Everest

Word Check

Choose the right picture for each word.

1 trash ______

2 light ______

3 climb ______

4 heavy ______

Grammar Check

Read and complete the sentences.

1 Jim is 30 kg. Ron is 35 kg. Alex is 38 kg.

➡ Alex is ______________ boy of the three. (heavy)

2 Daegu is 32˚C. Seoul is 28˚C. Sokcho is 25˚C.

➡ Daegu is ______________ city of the three. (hot)

3 The red bag is $30. The green bag is $50. The yellow bag is $38.

➡ The green bag is ______________ bag of the three. (expensive)

Comprehension Check

Read and choose the best answer.

1 Mt. Everest is the ____________ mountain in the world.

a highest

b coldest

c most beautiful

2 When climbers go up Mt. Everest, their bags are ____________________.

a full of trash

b light with nothing

c heavy with a lot of things

3 What is the heaviest thing in the climbers' bags?

a 

b 

c 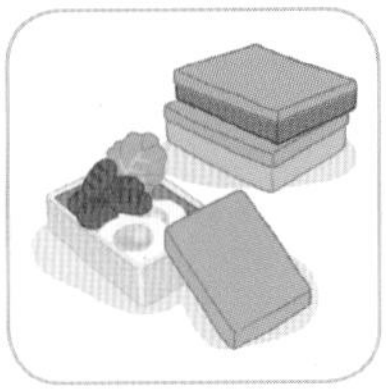

TRY IT

Read and choose the right word.

Nick : What's up? You look angry.
Katie: I read a story about Mt. Everest.
Nick : Mt. Everest? Is it the 1) ____________ mountain in the world?
Katie: That's right. A lot of people 2) ____________ it every year.
Sadly, they leave their 3) ____________ on Mt. Everest.
Nick : That's not good.

trash climb highest

STORY 02

Words to Learn

Look at the pictures and read the words.

scientist

cow

hurt

fart

burp

Grammar to Learn

Look at the picture and read the sentences.

The news is very funny.

How funny (the news is)!

What funny news (it is)!

Jay : How funny this news is! You won't believe it!

Ann: What's going on?

Jay : **Scientist**s say that **cow**s are **hurt**ing the Earth when they **fart** and **burp**.

Ann: You're joking!

Jay : No, it's true. A kind of gas comes out when they fart and burp. That gas is making the air too hot.

Ann: How interesting!

Jay : Yes. Scientists say that one cow makes about 280 liters of this gas a day.

Ann: That's a lot! What surprising news!

배경지식
호주에서 방목되는 소와 양 등 가축들의 방귀와 트림, 그리고 호흡을 통해 나오는 메탄 가스가 1년간 호주 전역에서 배출되는 온실 가스량의 5분의 1에 달한다는 주장이 나왔습니다.

MAIN IDEA ☆☆

The best title is ______________.

□ Cows Hurt the Earth

□ Cows' Interesting Habits

Word Check Match the words to the pictures.

1 scientist 2 fart 3 hurt 4 cow

Grammar Check Look at the examples and complete the sentences.

It is a very funny joke.
➡ What ___a funny joke it is___!

The building is very high.
➡ How ___high the building is___!

1 It is a very cute cat.
➡ What ______________________!

2 The game is very exciting.
➡ How ______________________!

Comprehension Check

Read and choose the best answer.

1 Cows are hurting the Earth when ________________.

a they eat grass

b they take showers

c they fart and burp

2 The gas from cows makes the air ________________.

a too hot

b too dirty

c too smelly

3 One cow makes about ________________ of gas a day.

a 180 liters

b 280 liters

c 380 liters

TRY IT

Complete the sentence with your own ideas.

We hurt the Earth when ________________________.

1) ________________________________

2) ________________________________

3) ________________________________

REVIEW TEST

[1~5] Look at the pictures and write the right words.

among	scientist	cow	burp	light

1 

2 

3 

4 

5 

[6~10] Choose and write the correct word.

6 Don't (fart / hot) in the room. It smells bad. ____________

7 He likes to (make / climb) high mountains. ____________

8 Don't leave any (air / trash) in the park. ____________

9 I put many books in the bag. The bag is (heavy / hot). ____________

10 Too many cars (hurt / burp) the Earth. ____________

[11~13] Write the words in the correct order.

11 (tallest, the, student)

➡ Bill is ____________________ in his class.

12 (is, dirty, the floor)

➡ How ____________________!

13 (beautiful pictures, they, are)!

➡ What ____________________!

[14~15] Read and answer.

Jay : __________ funny this news is! You won't believe it!
Ann: What's going on?
Jay : Scientists say that cows are hurting the Earth when they fart and burp.
Ann: You're joking!
Jay : No, it's true. A kind of gas comes out when they fart and burp. That gas is making the air too hot.
Ann: __________ interesting!
Jay : Yes. Scientists say that one cow makes about 280 liters of this gas a day.
Ann: That's a lot! What surprising news!

14 Write one word for both blanks.

____

15 Check True or False.

a Cows make the air too cold when they fart and burp. True False

b One cow makes about 280 liters of gas every month. True False

머리 식히는 영어 퍼즐

미션 : 규칙에 따라 같은 알파벳끼리 연결해 보세요!

규칙을 설명해 드리겠습니다!

- 모든 빈칸에는 1개의 선이 들어가야 합니다.
- 선끼리 교차할 수 없습니다.
- 같은 선으로 가로세로 연속된 2칸 모두(2x2 사각형 모양)를 채울 수는 없습니다.

[보기]

A	C		
			B
	C		B
			A

A	C		
			B
	C		B
			A

C			E			H
	E			H		
			G			
					A	
	F	C	G			
			F	B		
A						B

정답은 p.108에서 확인하세요.

UNIT 03

MY OPINION

Read and guess the stories.

STORY 01

Words to Learn

Look at the pictures and read the words.

hallway

enter

behave

record

uncomfortable

Grammar to Learn

Look at the picture and read the sentences.

The dress	**looks nice.**
The flower	**smells good.**
The pizza	**tastes yummy.**

Many schools have CCTV in their **hallways** and classrooms.
But do schools need CCTV?

Yes First, students can feel safe in school.
Bad people can't **enter** the school.
Second, students will not **behave** badly.
They know that CCTV can **record** all their actions.

No First, teachers and students can feel **uncomfortable**.
CCTV is always watching them.
Second, CCTV can't watch every place in school.
Bad things may still happen there.

MAIN IDEA ☆☆

The story is about ______________.

□ CCTV in school

□ CCTV on the street

Word Check Match the words to the pictures.

1 behave 2 enter 3 record 4 hallway

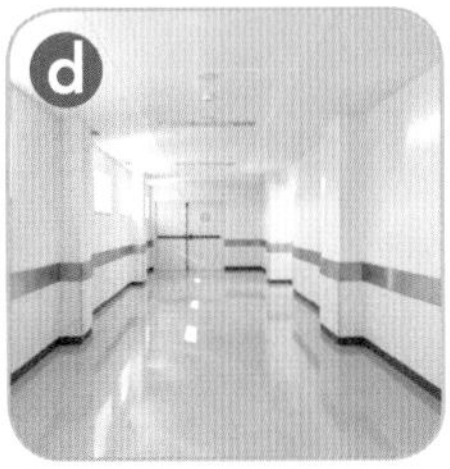

Grammar Check Circle the correct word for each sentence.

1 The bread feels (soft / softly).

2 The new chair looks (comfortable / comfortably).

3 The soap smells (good / well).

4 The idea sounds (interesting / interestingly).

5 The pizza tastes (delicious / deliciously).

Comprehension Check

Read and choose the best answer.

1 Why do some people want CCTV in school? (Choose two.)

a Students can feel safe.

b CCTV is not expensive.

c Students will not behave badly.

2 Some people don't want CCTV in school because they feel ____________.

a safe

b happy

c uncomfortable

3 CCTV can't watch every place in school, so ____________________.

a students should not go there

b bad things may happen there

c teachers don't need to watch it

TRY IT

Check yes or no and write your opinion in Korean.

Do schools need CCTV?

☐ YES	☐ NO

STORY 02

Words to Learn

Look at the pictures and read the words.

learn

draw

outside

lake

nature

miss

Grammar to Learn

Look at the pictures and read the sentences.

I	**always**	eat breakfast.
I	**never**	skip breakfast.

I	**usually**	read books at night.
I	**sometimes**	watch TV at night.

Usually, students study at school.

But John never goes to school.

He always **learn**s at home and other places.

He likes to **draw outside**.

His parents often take him to mountains and **lake**s.

He draws plants and animals there.

He goes to the library to read about **nature**.

He likes to visit art museums and look at paintings.

He sometimes **miss**es his friends.

But he thinks homeschooling has many good points.

MAIN IDEA ☆☆

The story is about ________________.

□ John's hobby

□ John's homeschooling

Word Check Choose the right picture for each word.

1 nature ______

2 draw ______

3 learn ______

4 miss ______

Grammar Check ☆ Read and choose the right word.

sometimes	always	often

1 I wake up late every day.
➡ I ____________ wake up late.

2 Ron eats breakfast twice a week.
➡ Ron ____________ eats breakfast.

3 When I was younger, I was sick a lot.
➡ When I was younger, I was ____________ sick.

Comprehension Check

Read and choose the best answer.

1 John's parents often take him to ______________.

a mountains and lakes

b theaters and museums

c gyms and a playground

2 John goes to the library to read about __________.

a art

b space

c nature

3 John likes to ______________________. (Choose two.)

a study at school

b visit art museums

c draw pictures outside

TRY IT

Read John's story and write your own opinions in Korean.

Q1: What is a good point of homeschooling?

Q2: What is a bad point of homeschooling?

REVIEW TEST

[1~5] Look at the pictures and write the right words.

uncomfortable	enter	draw	hallway	nature

1 

2 

3 

4 

5 

[6~10] Choose and write the correct word.

6 It is raining hard. Don't go (outside / side). ____________

7 Ann (felt / recorded) her son's dance. ____________

8 Minho (behaved / missed) his family very much. ____________

9 Cindy likes to (place / learn) English. ____________

10 The boys are swimming in the (lake / behave). ____________

[11~13] Choose the right words and complete the sentences.

looked	feel	sounded
sad	strong	tired

11 I didn't get enough sleep last night. Now I __________ __________.

12 Yesterday the music __________ __________. People cried a lot.

13 The man was holding the heavy box. He __________ __________.

[14~15] Read and answer.

Usually, students study at school.
But John __________ goes to school.
He always learns at home and other places.
He likes to draw outside.
His parents often take him to mountains and lakes.
He draws plants and animals there.
He goes to the library to read about nature.
He visits art museums and likes to walk around.
He sometimes misses his friends.
But he thinks homeschooling has many good points.

14 Choose the word for the blank.

a often

b never

c sometimes

15 Check True or False.

a John learns at home and other places. True False

b John doesn't miss his friends. True False

꼭 가봐야 할 환상적인 여행지

영화나 광고에서 감탄을 자아내는 풍경들이 실제로 있다? 없다? 있다!!!

몰디브에는 별의 바다(Sea of Stars)가 있다!

몰디브 바드후 섬의 바다는 밤이 되면 바다 안에 별이 있는 것처럼 반짝입니다. 그 이유는 빛을 내는 플랑크톤들이 해변으로 몰려들기 때문이라고 하네요. 은하수 같은 광경이 바다에서 펼쳐진다고 하니 매우 아름답겠죠?

볼리비아에는 투명한 소금 사막이 있다!

볼리비아의 우유니 소금사막은 하늘과 땅이 구분되지 않을 정도로 투명하여 신비한 사진을 찍을 수 있습니다. 원래는 바다였던 이곳은 지각변동으로 솟아올라 호수가 되었고, 건조한 기후 때문에 물이 모두 증발하여 소금 알갱이만 남게 되었다고 하네요.

미국에는 빛의 아름다움을 볼 수 있는 협곡이 있다!

미국 애리조나 주에는 사진작가들에게 '눈, 마음 그리고 영혼에 축복을 내리는 장소'라고 불리는 아름다운 협곡이 있습니다. 바로 앤털로프 캐니언인데요. 이곳에서는 주황, 노랑부터 파랑, 보라에 이르기까지, 빛에 따라 다양한 색을 선사하는 협곡의 모습을 볼 수 있습니다. 협곡의 벽에 일렁이는 빛의 아름다움이 환상적인 광경을 선사한다고 하네요.

UNIT 04
SHOPPING
Read and guess the stories.
When you buy chocolate, check for the fair trade sign.
Okay.
This cart is heavy. It makes me move slowly.

STORY 01

Words to Learn

Look at the pictures and read the words.

cart

way

reason

full

push

secret

Grammar to Learn

Look at the picture and read the sentences.

People	**called him Hulk.**
A bad guy	**made him angry.**
Hulk	**made the bad guy fall down.**

Malls try to make people buy more things.

Carts are one **way** of doing this.

Malls make them big and heavy for special **reason**s.

First, if a cart is not **full**, people feel they buy little.

So they put more things into it.

Second, people can't **push** heavy carts fast.

They move slowly and buy more things.

Big and heavy carts are the big **secret** for malls.

MAIN IDEA☆☆

The story is about ________________.

□ the new shopping mall

□ the secret of carts in the mall

Word Check

Choose the right picture for each word.

1 secret ______

2 full ______

3 way ______

4 reason ______

a 

b 

c 

d 

Grammar Check

Circle the correct word for each sentence.

1 The music made me (sad / sadly).

2 Jim always makes people (to laugh / laugh).

3 The book made him (famous / famously).

4 This sauce can make any food (delicious / deliciously).

5 My teacher made us (to do / do) a lot of homework.

Comprehension Check

Read and choose the best answer.

1 Malls try to ______________________.

a make a lot of new things

b make carts light and small

c make people buy more things

2 If a cart is not full, ______________________.

a people want to buy little

b malls make the shelves full

c people put more things into it

3 Malls make carts heavy, so ______________________.

a people can push them safely

b people can't move them fast

c they want to make them stronger

TRY IT

Read and fill in the blanks.

Causes		Effects
Malls make carts big.	➡	People feel they buy 1) __________.
Malls make carts heavy.	➡	People push them 2) __________.
		⬇⬇
		People buy 3) __________ things.

STORY 02

Words to Learn Look at the pictures and read the words.

look for

flavor

price

be made from

cheaply

fair

Grammar to Learn Look at the picture and read the sentences.

When	it is hot, turn on the air conditioner.
If	the window is open, close it.
Because	the air conditioner is on, it will be cool soon.

When you buy chocolate, what do you **look for**?

Flavor? The **price**?

Why don't you look for the Fair Trade sign?

Chocolate **is made from** cocoa beans.

Farmers work long hours.

But big companies buy cocoa beans from them too **cheaply**.

Because some think this is not **fair**, a new company started.

It buys cocoa beans at a fair price. The farmers get more money.

If you buy chocolate with the Fair Trade sign,

you can help make the world better.

MAIN IDEA ☆☆

The story is about ______________.

☐ cheap chocolate

☐ Fair Trade chocolate

Word Check

Match the words to the pictures.

1 price 2 fair 3 flavor 4 cheaply

Grammar Check

Circle the correct word for each sentence.

1 I lived in the US (when / if) I was a child.

2 Last night, Tom went to bed early (if / because) he was sick.

3 I was busy (if / when) Joy called me.

4 (Because / If) you have a question, please ask me.

5 Susan is sad (because / if) her puppy is missing.

6 (If / Because) I meet Minsu, I will be very happy.

Comprehension Check

Read and choose the best answer.

1 Chocolate is made from ______________.

a peanuts

b cocoa beans

c coffee beans

2 Farmers work __________ hours, but they get __________ money from big companies.

a long – little

b long – more

c short – more

3 If we buy chocolate with ______________, we can help make the world better.

a a price mark

b a flavor mark

c the Fair Trade sign

TRY IT

Read and fill in the blanks.

Problems		Solution		Results
Farmers work 1) __________ hours. Big companies buy cocoa beans too 2) __________.	➡	Fair Trade	➡	A new company buys cocoa beans at a 3) __________ price. Farmers get 4) __________ money.

REVIEW TEST

[1 ~ 5] Look at the pictures and write the right words.

price	push	cart	reason	fair

1

2

3

4

5

[6 ~ 10] Choose and write the correct word.

6 The room is (full / heavy) of toys. ____________

7 Lily doesn't want to tell her (make / secret). ____________

8 My favorite (price / flavor) of ice cream is chocolate. ____________

9 Cheese (looks for / is made from) milk. ____________

10 I bought the car (cheaply / company). ____________

[11~12] Choose the right word.

when	because

11 ___________ I have a test tomorrow, I have to study.

12 ___________ you buy fish, check the color of their eyes.

[13~14] Read and answer.

When you buy chocolate, what do you look for?
Flavor? The price?
Why don't you look for the Fair Trade sign?
Chocolate is made from cocoa beans.
Farmers work long hours.
But big companies buy cocoa beans from them too cheaply.
Because some think this is not fair, a new company started.
It buys cocoa beans at a fair price. The farmers get more money.
If you buy chocolate with the Fair Trade sign, you can help
_________________.

13 Check True or False.

a Big companies buy cocoa beans at a fair price. True False

b After a new company started, the farmers get more money. True False

14 Choose the phrase for the blank.

a make the world better

b make the new company rich

c make farmers get more cocoa beans

신기하게 생긴 식물들

꽃봉오리 모자를 쓴 사람 같아 보이는
이 꽃은 오루키스 이탈리카 입니다.
우리말로 해석하면 이탈리아 남성
야생 난초입니다.
당장에라도 걸어 나올 것 같죠?
지중해 연안에 분포한다고 합니다.

플라잉 오리 난초라는 이 꽃은
까만 새끼 오리가 날고 있는 것처럼
보입니다.
만화영화 캐릭터인 '대피덕'을 똑
닮았죠?
호주가 원산지인 이 꽃의 길이는
1.5cm 정도라고 합니다.

이것은 알리스톨로치아 살바도렌시스
라는 꽃으로 스타워즈(Star Wars)의
다스 베이더를 닮았습니다.
흰색 부분은 두 눈처럼 보이고
가운데에 불룩하게 솟아오른 것은
코의 모양과 같죠?
꽃의 내부에는 아래로 향한 털이
빼곡히 돋아있는데 그곳에 곤충이
갇히기도 합니다.

UNIT 05
GOOD INVENTIONS
Read and guess the stories.
Wow, that looks like an airplane! What is it?
It's a drone.
I enjoy dancing. I want to dance in the box, too.

STORY 01

Words to Learn

Look at the pictures and read the words.

normal

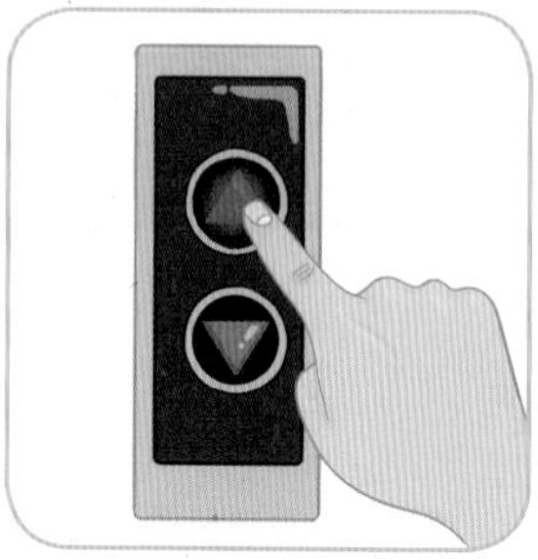

press

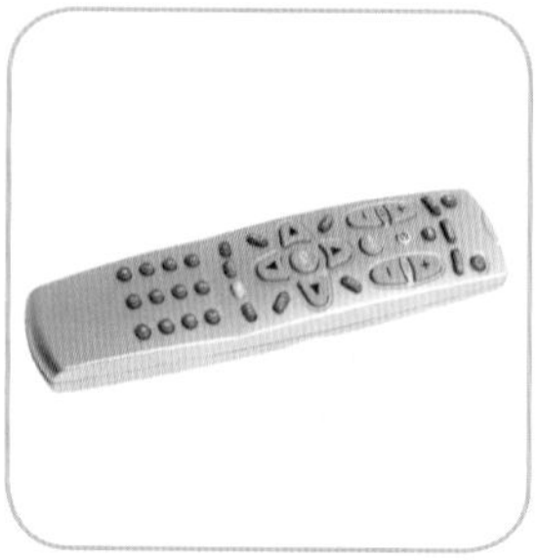

remote control

pick up

technology

convenient

Grammar to Learn

Look at the pictures and read the sentences.

The restaurant	looks	nice.
It	looks like	an airplane.

This bread	tastes	delicious.
It	tastes like	pizza.

A new shoe store opened.

It looks **normal**, but it is different.

Usually people use a ladder to reach the shoes on the top shelves.

But here, drones carry the shoes.

A clerk **press**es a button on a **remote control**.

Then, a drone flies to **pick up** the shoes.

They look like airplanes. But there is no pilot.

Technology makes shopping more **convenient**.

> **배경지식**
> 드론(drone)은 리모컨으로 조종하는 무인 비행기를 가리킵니다. 현재 사진 및 영상 촬영, 물건 배달 등 다양한 용도로 쓰이고 있습니다. 앞으로 일상적으로 드론을 볼 수 있을 것입니다.

MAIN IDEA ☆☆

The best title is ______________.

□ The Shoe Store with Pilots

□ The Shoe Store with Drones

Word Check Match the words to the pictures.

1 convenient 2 press 3 remote control 4 pick up

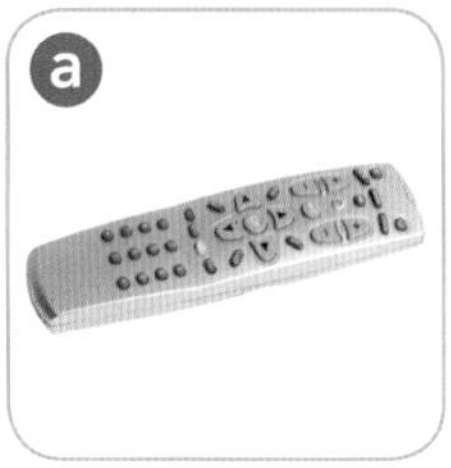

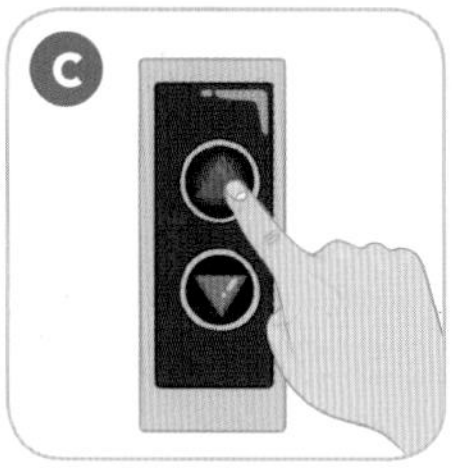

Grammar Check Circle the correct word for each sentence.

1 The shoes (look / look like) comfortable.

2 The robots (look / look like) men.

3 The soup (tastes / tastes like) curry.

4 The tea (tastes / tastes like) good.

5 The candle (smells / smells like) roses.

Comprehension Check

Read and choose the best answer.

1 The drones fly to ______________.

a bring ladders
b pick up the shoes
c take people to the top shelves

2 The drones look like __________.

a shoes
b people
c airplanes

3 The clerks control the drones with the ______________.

a computer
b smartphone
c remote control

TRY IT

Read and choose the right words.

Smart Shoe Store

Our shoe store is different.
We don't have 1) __________.
But we can reach the shoes on the top shelves.
Just 2) ______________ on the remote control!
And a drone gets your shoes.
Shopping in our store is 3) __________.

ladders	convenient	press the button

STORY 02

Words to Learn

Look at the pictures and read the words.

across

invent

traffic light

side

copy

Grammar to Learn

Look at the pictures and read the sentences.

I	**enjoy watching**	movies.
I	**finished doing**	my homework.
I	**kept eating**	popcorn.

I	**want to learn**	Chinese.
I	**decided to study**	Chinese hard.
I	**needed to buy**	some books.

Some people walk **across** the road at red lights.

They are busy or simply don't want to wait.

But it is dangerous.

One company wanted to make waiting fun.

So it **invent**ed a dancing **traffic light**!

On one **side** of the road, a person dances in a special box.

The red light **copies** the dance.

Across the road, people enjoy watching the dancing light.

They enjoy waiting!

This great idea made the city safer.

배경지식

한 자동차 회사가 포르투갈 리스본에 춤추는 빨간 신호등을 설치했습니다. 이 신호등 덕분에, 횡단보도에서 신호를 지키는 비율이 이전보다 81% 증가했다고 합니다.

MAIN IDEA ☆☆

The best title is ____________________.

□ The Dancing City

□ The Dancing Traffic Light

Word Check Choose the right picture for each word.

1 side ______ 2 copy ______ 3 invent ______ 4 traffic light ______

Grammar Check Circle the correct word for each sentence.

1 I want (to know / knowing) about it.

2 Jake enjoys (to dance / dancing) in front of people.

3 Hyuna finished (to read / reading) the book.

4 I need (to see / seeing) you soon.

5 They decided (to do / doing) their homework first.

Comprehension Check

Read and choose the best answer.

1 One company wanted to make waiting for traffic lights __________.

a fun

b healthy

c strange

2 The red light copies __________________ in a special box.

a a person's face

b a person's song

c a person's dance

3 The dancing traffic light made the city __________.

a safer

b more boring

c more dangerous

TRY IT

Read and fill in the blanks.

Problem	People walk across the road at 1) __________.
Solution	One company invented a 2) __________ traffic light.
Result	People now enjoy 3) __________. The city is safer.

REVIEW TEST

[1~5] Look at the pictures and write the right words.

press　　across　　invent　　convenient　　copy

1

2

3

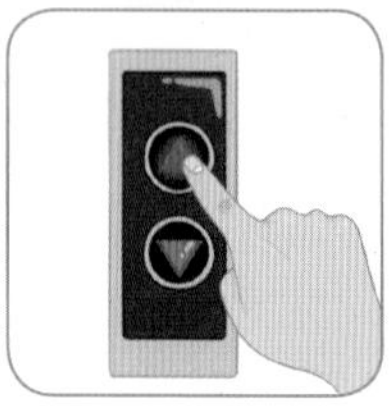

4

5

[6~10] Choose and write the correct words.

6 Look at the (ladder / traffic light) when you cross the road. ____________

7 This looks (normal / copy), but it has many special uses. ____________

8 I turned on the TV with the (copy / remote control). ____________

9 (Technology / Side) makes our life convenient. ____________

10 I (invented / picked up) the trash on the street. ____________

[11~12] Choose the right words.

11 | look | looks | looks like

He ___________ a different person.

12 | eat | eating | to eat

James wants ___________ ice cream.

[13~14] Read and answer.

A new shoe store opened.
It looks normal, but it is different.
Usually people use a ladder to reach the shoes on the top shelves.
But here, drones carry the shoes.
A clerk presses a button on a remote control.
Then, a drone flies to pick up the shoes.
They look like airplanes. But there is no pilot.
Technology makes shopping _______________.

13 Choose the word(s) for the blank.

- **a** safer
- **b** more dangerous
- **c** more convenient

14 Check True or False.

a This store looks different from other stores.	True	False
b People use ladders in this shoe store.	True	False
c Clerks fly to pick up the shoes.	True	False

많이 사용하는 영어 줄임말

다음 대화의 밑줄 친 부분의 뜻이 무엇인지 맞혀보세요.

[정답]

OMG: 'Oh, my god!'의 줄임말로 '이럴 수가!'의 의미입니다.

NP: 'No problem.'의 줄임말로 '괜찮다. 문제 없다.'의 의미입니다.

BFF:는 'best friend forever'의 줄임말로 '영원한 절친'의 의미입니다.

CU: 'See you.'의 줄임말로 헤어질 때 하는 인사말입니다.

UNIT 06
TECHNOLOGY
Read and guess the stories.
Wash your hands first. Your hands may be dirty.
You may touch this picture.
What are you doing?
I am turning off my TV.

STORY 01

Words to Learn

Look at the pictures and read the words.

sign

painting

rule

visitor

blind

Grammar to Learn

Look at the pictures and read the sentences.

She	**may like**	this art museum.
He	**may not like**	this art museum.

You	**may touch**	the paintings.
You	**may not take**	pictures here.

You may often see this **sign** in art museums:

"Don't touch the **painting**s."

But the **rule** is different in this 3D museum.

Visitors may touch the paintings!

3D printers made them.

People may touch Mona Lisa's face.

They can feel her smile by touch.

This is good news for **blind** people.

Until now, they could not enjoy the paintings.

3D technology brings them happiness.

But the paintings may not be so clean!

> **배경지식**
> 스페인 마드리드에 있는 프라도 미술관에서는 시각 장애인들이 미술 작품을 감상할 수 있도록 하기 위해 몇몇 작품을 3D 프린터로 복제하여 전시했습니다. 작품을 색다르게 느낄 수 있어 시각 장애인 뿐만 아니라 비장애인들에게도 인기가 있다고 합니다.

MAIN IDEA ☆☆

The story is about ________________.

☐ the Mona Lisa

☐ a 3D museum

Word Check Choose the right picture for each word.

1 rule ______ 2 sign ______ 3 visitor ______ 4 painting ______

Grammar Check Write the meaning of 'may' for each sentence.

1 You may use my smartphone. ______

2 She may like this action movie. ______

3 You may not watch TV too much. ______

4 They may be middle school students. ______

5 May I touch this picture? ______

Comprehension Check

Read and choose the best answer.

1 In the 3D museum, the rule is __________ from the rule in other museums.

a different
b the same
c interesting

2 ______________ helps blind people enjoy the paintings.

a The signs
b Mona Lisa
c 3D technology

3 The paintings may not be __________ in the 3D museum.

a safe
b cold
c clean

TRY IT

Read and circle the right word.

How to Enjoy Paintings

In the 3D museum	In other art museums
People 1) (may / may not) touch the paintings. People 2) (can / cannot) feel the paintings.	People 3) (may / may not) touch the paintings. People 4) (can / cannot) look at the paintings.

STORY 02

Words to Learn

Look at the pictures and read the words.

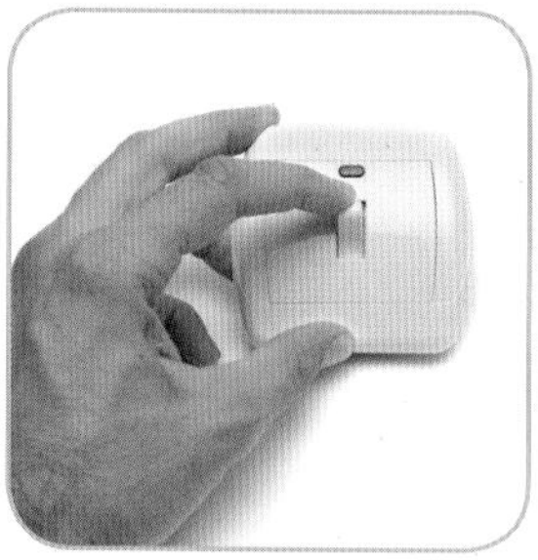

turn off

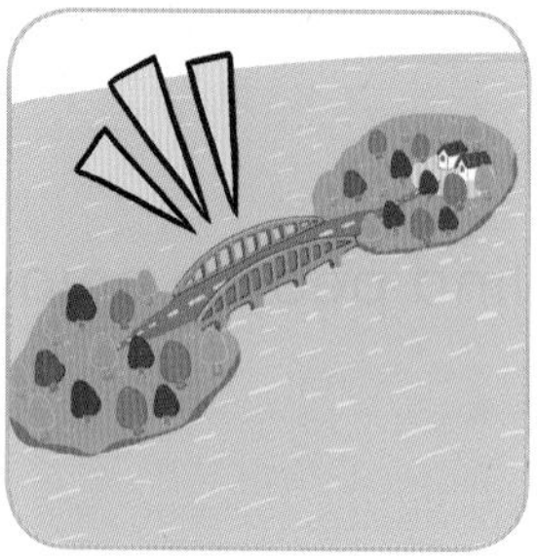

connect

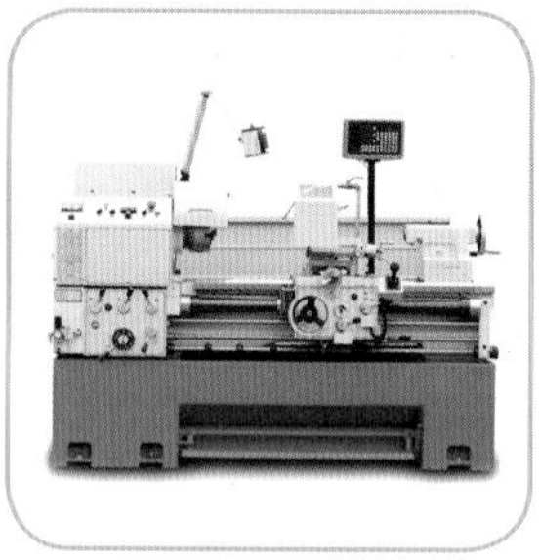

machine

control

break down

Grammar to Learn

Look at the pictures and read the sentences.

I	**am**	a teacher.
He	**is**	a cook.
They	**are**	dancers.

I	**am teaching**	now.
He	**is cooking**	now.
They	**are dancing**	now.

Jenny is eating at a restaurant.

Her smartphone rings. It is a message from her home.

It says, "You left your heating on."

She uses her phone to **turn off** her heating.

The Internet is **connect**ing all **machine**s together.

People call this the Internet of Things(IoT).

With this, you can **control** things with your smartphone.

It makes our life convenient. But there is a problem.

If a virus attacks, all machines will **break down**.

MAIN IDEA ☆☆

The story is about ___________________.

□ the Internet of Things

□ the viruses of the Internet

Word Check Match the words to the pictures.

1 machine 2 break down 3 connect 4 control

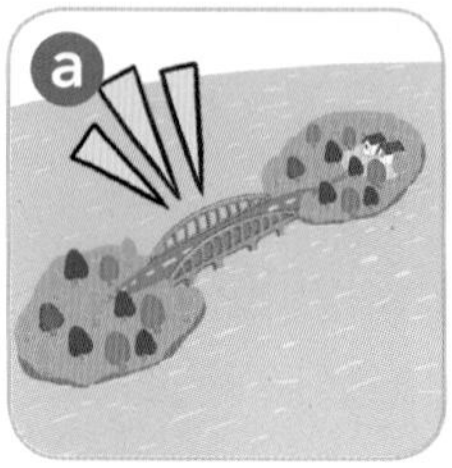

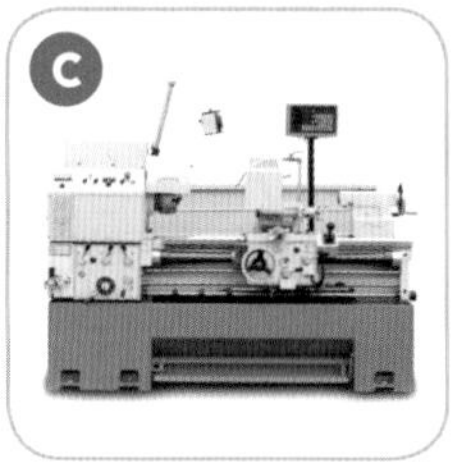

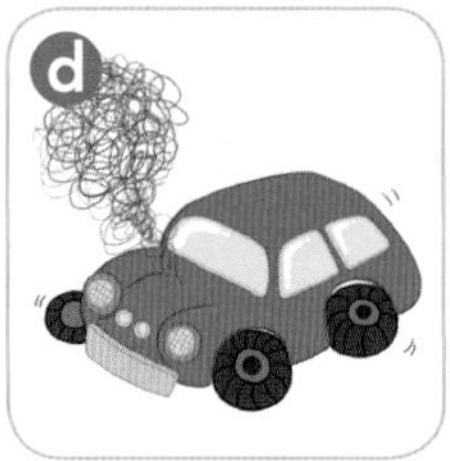

Grammar Check Look at the example and complete the sentences.

I talk on the phone.
➡ I ___am talking___ on the phone now.

1 My father drives a red car.
➡ My father ________________ a red car now.

2 They study Chinese.
➡ They ________________ Chinese now.

3 My sisters eat fruit.
➡ My sisters ________________ fruit now.

Comprehension Check

Read and choose the best answer.

1 How did Jenny turn off her heating?

a 

b 

c 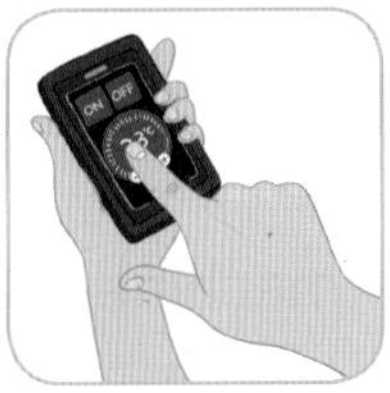

2 The __________ connects all machines together.

a wire

b Internet

c telephone

3 All the machines will break down if __________.

a a virus attacks

b a thief attacks

c a robot attacks

TRY IT

Read and choose the right words.

The Internet of Things

Good Points	Bad Points
You can 1) __________ machines with a smartphone. It makes our life 2) __________.	Machines can 3) __________ if there is a virus.

break down	control	convenient

REVIEW TEST

[1~5] Look at the pictures and write the right words.

blind	machine	visitor	painting	break down

1

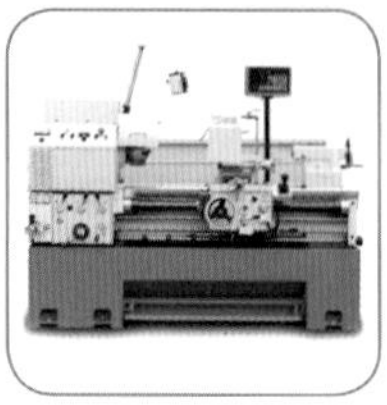

2

3

4

5

[6~10] Choose and write the correct words.

6 (Rule / Turn off) the phone in the classroom. ____________

7 The bridge (connects / attacks) the two cities. ____________

8 You should follow our (paintings / rules) here. ____________

9 I can (sign / control) the robot with my smartphone. ____________

10 The (sign / visitor) on the wall says, "Don't touch." ____________

[11~12] Change the words and fill in the blanks.

11 Jinho ________________ English now. (study)

12 Sora ________________ computer games now. (play)

[13~14] Read and answer.

Jenny is eating at a restaurant.
Her smartphone rings. It is a message from her home.
It says, "You left your heating on."
She uses her phone to turn off her heating.
The Internet is connecting all machines together.
People call this the Internet of Things(IoT).
With this, you can control things with your smartphone.
It makes our life convenient. But there is a(n) __________.
If a virus attacks, all machines will break down.

13 Choose the word for the blank.

a answer

b question

c problem

14 Check True or False.

a Jenny can only turn off her heating at home.	True	False
b The machines will never break down.	True	False

뇌가 당신을 말해준다

Q. 무심코 깍지를 꼈을 때,
어느 쪽 엄지 손가락이
밑에 있나요?

왼손이 밑에 있다면? 좌뇌
오른손이 밑에 있다면? 우뇌

Q. 무심코 팔짱을 꼈을 때,
어느 쪽 팔이 밑에 있나요?
(손등이 아니라 팔의 위치를
살펴보세요.)

왼팔이 밑에 있다면? 좌뇌
오른팔이 밑에 있다면? 우뇌

첫 번째 테스트와 두 번째 테스트의 결과를 합해 보세요! 당신의 뇌는 무슨 형인가요?
나의 뇌가 무슨 형인지 알았다면 나는 어떤 타입의 사람인지 아래의 글을 읽어보세요.

[좌좌뇌형] ▶ 꼼꼼하고 성실한 타입!

당신은 성실하며 의리가 있어
주위 사람들로부터 신뢰를 얻습니다.
하지만 융통성이 부족하네요.

[좌우뇌형] ▶ 자상한 형님/누나 타입!

당신은 남 챙기는 것을 좋아합니다.
머리 회전이 빠르고 타고난 센스가 있어
상대의 기분을 빨리 파악합니다.

[우좌뇌형] ▶ 정도 많고 인기도 많은 리더 타입!

당신은 집단을 잘 이끄는 사람입니다.
주위 사람들은 당신을 신뢰하고 잘 따릅니다.
다만 화를 잘 못내고 남의 부탁을 거절하지
못한다는 단점이 있네요.

[우우뇌형] ▶ 낙천적이고 개성 넘치는 타입!

당신은 호기심이 많고 도전도 좋아합니다.
사람들 사이에서 분위기도 잘 띄울 수 있죠.
좋아하는 일에는 미친듯이 매진하지만,
관심이 없는 것은 거들떠보지도 않네요.

UNIT 07
IN SPACE
Read and guess the stories.
I have to be careful. I must tie myself to my bed.
Turn down the volume! That sound cannot be real.

STORY 01

Words to Learn Look at the pictures and read the words.

astronaut

space

float

spaceship

tie

Grammar to Learn Look at the picture and read the sentences.

I / You / We / They	must have to	be careful.		He / She	must has to	be careful.

Jane is an **astronaut**.

She sometimes travels into **space**.

In space, she needs to eat, sleep, and use the bathroom.

When she eats, she must be careful.

If not, her food can **float** around in the **spaceship**.

When she sleeps, she must **tie** herself to her bed.

She also has to tie herself to the toilet in the bathroom.

It's a little difficult, but she is happy.

She can see the beautiful Earth every day.

MAIN IDEA ☆☆

The best title is ______________.

☐ Life in Space

☐ Life at School

Word Check Match the words to the pictures.

1 spaceship 2 tie 3 float 4 astronaut

a 
b 
c 
d 

Grammar Check Look at the pictures and complete the sentences.

I __must__ wear a helmet.
= I __have__ __to__ wear a helmet.

1 You ________ be quiet in the library.
= You ________ ________ be quiet in the library.

2 He ________ be careful at the crosswalk.
= He ________ ________ be careful at the crosswalk.

Comprehension Check Read and choose the best answer.

1 The life in space is __________.

a easy
b boring
c difficult

2 What do astronauts do when they go to sleep?

a They wear special clothes.
b They sleep in a special case.
c They tie themselves to their bed.

3 Jane is happy to see ________________ every day.

a the beautiful stars
b the beautiful Earth
c the beautiful friends

TRY IT Read and fill in the blanks.

Life in Space

Food	➡	Q: Why do they eat carefully? A: Food can 1) __________ in the spaceship.
Sleep	➡	Q: How can they go to sleep? A: They 2) __________ themselves to their bed.
Bathroom	➡	Q: How can they use the bathroom? A: They 3) __________ themselves to the toilet.

STORY 02

Words to Learn

Look at the pictures and read the words.

turn on

shoot

loud

silent

turn down

Grammar to Learn

Look at the picture and read the sentences.

The movie	**must**	be wrong.
People	must	wear special clothes in space.
The movie	**cannot**	be real.
People	cannot	live without special clothes in space.

Turn on the TV. It's time to watch *Star Wars*.

You must listen to the sounds. Boom! Zap! Bam!

Two spaceships are **shoot**ing at each other.

It is very **loud**.

But these sounds cannot be real!

Moving air makes sound, but there is no air in space.

That means space is **silent**.

The sounds in *Star Wars* cannot happen.

Next time you watch *Star Wars*, **turn down** the volume!

MAIN IDEA☆☆

The story is about ______________.

☐ movies in space

☐ sounds in space

Word Check Choose the right picture for each word.

1 shoot ______ 2 silent ______ 3 loud ______ 4 turn down ______

Grammar Check Circle the correct word for each sentence.

1 He didn't come to school today. He (must / cannot) be sick.

2 They are sleeping. They (must / cannot) use the computer.

3 The story (must / cannot) be true. I don't believe it!

4 She (must / cannot) be watching TV now. She always watches TV.

5 *Star Wars* (must / cannot) be very exciting. Everyone likes it.

Comprehension Check

Read and choose the best answer.

1 Loud sounds in *Star Wars* _______________.

a can happen

b must be real

c cannot be real

2 _______________ makes sound.

a Moving air

b Moving stars

c Moving spaceships

3 There is _______________ in space, so there is no sound.

a no TV

b no air

c too much air

TRY IT

Read the dialog and fill in the blank.

Sue: What are you doing?

Sam: I'm watching *Star Wars*. Its sounds are very loud!

Sue: If you want to feel the real sound of space, you should _______________.

REVIEW TEST

[1~5] Look at the pictures and write the right words.

space	shoot	tie	astronaut	loud

1

2

3

4

5

[6~10] Choose and write the correct words.

6 It's too loud. (Turn down / Tie) the volume. ____________

7 Astronauts travel in a (toilet / spaceship). ____________

8 No one speaks in the room. The room is (silent / shoot). ____________

9 A red balloon is (floating / shooting) in the air. ____________

10 The room was dark, so I (turned on / turned down) the light. ____________

[11~13] Choose the right words.

must	cannot	has to

11 She just had lunch. She __________ be hungry now.

12 Jinsu studied English very hard. He __________ get good marks.

13 Joe is in the library. She __________ be quiet.

[14~15] Read and answer.

Jane is an __________.
She sometimes travels into space.
In space, she needs to eat, sleep, and use the bathroom.
When she eats, she must be careful.
If not, her food float around in the spaceship.
When she sleeps, she must tie herself to her bed.
She also has to tie herself to the toilet
in the bathroom.
It's a little difficult, but she is happy.
She can see the beautiful Earth every day.

14 Choose the word for the blank.

a pilot

b student

c astronaut

15 Check True or False.

a In space, Jane doesn't need to sleep. True False

b Jane is unhappy because she can't see the Earth. True False

Quiz 잠자는 뇌를 깨워주는 퀴즈

친구와 함께 아래의 문제들을 풀어보세요!

Q1. 직선을 하나만 그어 아래의 식이 성립되게 하세요.
두 가지 식에는 같은 규칙이 적용됩니다.
(단, 등호(=)는 건드리지 마세요.)

4+4+4 = 448

5+5+5 = 550

Q2. 여섯 장의 숫자 카드가 있습니다.
규칙을 찾아 물음표에 들어갈 숫자를 구하세요.

16	06	68	88	?	98

[정답]
Q1. 4+4의 +(더하기)부분에 직선을 하나 그으면 4가 됩니다.
따라서 444+4=448
마찬가지로 5+5의 +(더하기)부분에 직선을 하나 그으면 4가 됩니다.
따라서 545+5=550
Q2. 78
책의 위 아래를 뒤집어 보면 일정한 규칙이 보입니다.
86 ? 88 89 90 91이라는 숫자의 규칙이 보이시죠?

UNIT 08
TRADITIONS

Read and guess the stories.

STORY 01

Words to Learn Look at the pictures and read the words.

doll

worry

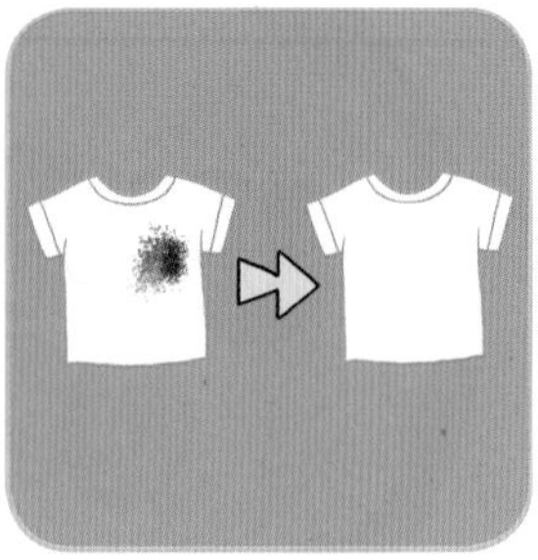

take away

pillow

disappear

Grammar to Learn Look at the picture and read the sentences.

I	tell David my worries.
I	tell my worries to David.

Lucy has a **doll**.

It looks sad, but it has a special power.

When she tells it her **worries**, it **take**s them **away**.

It's a traditional Mayan doll.

Mayan people told dolls their worries.

And then they put the dolls under their **pillow**s at night.

The dolls took away their worries.

Lucy told her worries to her doll like Mayan people did.

She hopes her worries **disappear** by the morning.

Think!

What do you want to tell a Mayan doll?

1. ____________

2. ____________

MAIN IDEA ☆☆

The best title is ____________.

☐ A Special Doll

☐ A Special Worry

Word Check Match the words to the pictures.

1 pillow

2 doll

3 worry

4 disappear

Grammar Check Look at the example and complete the sentences.

My brother told me his secret.

➡ My brother ___told his secret to me___.

1 I will tell you my story.

➡ I will ______________________.

2 My teacher told us the news.

➡ My teacher ______________________.

Comprehension Check

Read and choose the best answer.

1 What is Lucy's doll?

a 

b 

c 

2 At night, Mayan people put the traditional dolls ______________.

a under their beds

b under their pillows

c under their blankets

3 Traditional Mayan dolls took away people's __________.

a secrets

b worries

c dreams

TRY IT

Number the sentences in the correct order.

When Lucy has worries, what happens?

1) ______ Lucy puts the doll under the pillow.

2) ______ Lucy tells her worry to the doll.

3) ______ The doll takes away Lucy's worry.

STORY 02

Words to Learn

Look at the pictures and read the words.

hang from

cliff

hold onto

honey

hive

fall

Grammar to Learn

Look at the pictures and read the sentences.

Jake's hobby is **baking** cookies.

Baking cookies is fun.

He likes **baking** cookies.

Katie **is making** cookies.

She **is adding** chocolate chips.

A long rope ladder **hangs from** the top of a **cliff**.

A man is **holding onto** the ladder.

His job is collecting **honey**.

He uses long sticks to get the honey.

It is the best honey in the world.

But getting the honey is not easy

because the **hive**s are on a cliff.

It is very dangerous.

Only the ladder can keep him from **fall**ing.

This is a traditional job in Nepal.

배경지식

네팔의 꿀 사냥은 세계에서 가장 큰 벌집과 품질 좋은 야생 벌꿀을 얻을 수 있기 때문에 수 천년 동안 이어지고 있는 전통입니다. 하지만 가파른 절벽에서 줄에 의존하여 꿀 사냥을 하는 것은 매우 위험하고, 지구의 기후 변화로 인해 꿀벌이 점차 감소함에 따라 전통이 사라질 위기에 이르렀습니다.

MAIN IDEA ☆☆

The story is about ________________.

☐ a popular job in Nepal

☐ a traditional job in Nepal

Word Check
Choose the right picture for each word.

1 hive ______ 2 cliff ______ 3 fall ______ 4 hold onto ______

Grammar Check
Circle the correct word for each sentence.

1 His job is (driving / to driving) a bus.

2 (Drink / Drinking) water is good for your health.

3 Mary likes (study / studying) English.

4 (Selling / To selling) toys is his job.

5 Her hobby is (go / going) to the movies.

Comprehension Check Read and choose the best answer.

1 The man's job is ______________.

a collecting honey

b protecting bees

c making rope ladders

2 Where is the hive?

a 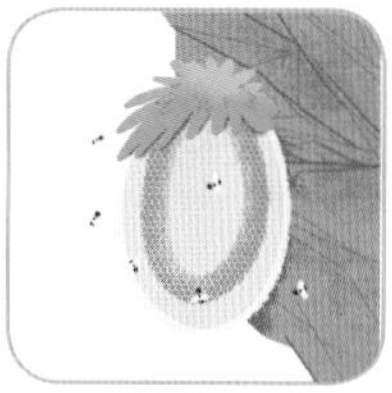

b 

c 

3 What keeps the man from falling?

a long sticks

b a rope ladder

c special clothes

TRY IT Read and choose the right words.

Honey Collecting Tour

You can be a honey collector.
It is a 1) ______________ job in Nepal.
You can get the best 2) ______________ in the world.
The hives are on 3) ______________, so you will use
4) ______________.
It is dangerous but amazing.

cliffs
honey
traditional
a rope ladder

REVIEW TEST

[1~5] Look at the pictures and write the right words.

disappear	hold onto	hive	doll	fall

1 

2 

3 

4 

5 

[6~10] Choose and write the correct word.

6 I use a high (ladder / pillow) when I sleep. ____________

7 My English test is a big (worry / hive) for me. ____________

8 I added some (honey / doll) to the juice. ____________

9 The man is climbing a (cliff / job). ____________

10 This medicine will (take away / fall) the pain. ____________

[11~13] Correct the underlined words.

11 Play soccer is fun. ______________________

12 My hobby is collect comic books. ______________________

13 I will tell my secrets him. ______________________

[14~15] Read and answer.

Lucy has a doll.
It looks sad, but it has a special power.
When she tells it her worries, it takes them away.
It's a traditional Mayan doll.
Mayan people told dolls their worries.
And then they put the dolls under their pillows at night.
The dolls took away their worries.
Lucy told her worries to her doll like Mayan people did.
She hopes her worries __________ by the morning.

14 Choose the word for the blank.

a appear
b disappear
c come back

15 Check True or False.

a A Mayan doll looks sad, but it has a special power. True False
b A Mayan doll makes people worry. True False

재미있는 동물 심리 테스트

Q1. 당신은 아프리카를 여행 중입니다. 마을 사람 중 한 명이 당신에게 양, 원숭이, 소, 사자, 말을 다른 마을로 이동시켜 달라고 부탁하여 동물들을 데리고 이동 중이죠.
하지만 점점 지치게 되어 딱! 한 마리의 동물만 버리고 가기로 합니다.
당신은 어떤 동물을 버릴 건가요?

① 양 ② 원숭이 ③ 소 ④ 사자 ⑤ 말

이 질문의 답은 나는 힘들고 지칠 때 무엇을 가장 먼저 버리는지를 이야기해 줍니다.
①양-사랑 ②원숭이-친구 ③소-직업
④사자-자존심 ⑤말-가족

Q2. 당신은 친구와 함께 길을 걷던 중, 마법사를 만나게 됩니다.
마법사는 당신을 여우로 변신시키고, 당신의 친구도 어떤 동물로 변신시켰습니다.
당신의 친구는 어떤 동물로 변신했을까요?

① 곰 ② 사슴 ③ 다람쥐 ④ 토끼

이 질문의 답은 나의 질투심의 정도를 이야기해 줍니다.
① 곰 - 질투심이 낮다. 피곤하게 살지 않는 타입.
② 사슴 - 질투심이 매우 낮다. 질투보다 남을 축하해주는 편이다.
③ 다람쥐 - 질투심이 강하다. 남이 잘 되는 것을 싫어한다.
④ 토끼 - 질투심이 다소 있다. 자신은 질투를 안 한다고 생각할 뿐!

초등학생의 영어 친구

리딩버디

정답 및 해석

3

UNIT 01 MONEY

STORY 01 PP.8~11

Words to Learn

clerk: 점원　stone: 돌　thankfully: 고맙게도
carry: 들고 다니다　owner: 주인, 소유자

Grammar to Learn

이 돌은 나만큼 크다.
이 돌은 나의 가방만큼 작다.

직독직해 P.9

When / you buy something, / you ask / "How much is it?"
~할 때 / 당신이 무엇인가를 사다 / 당신은 묻는다 / 이것은 얼마인가요
Then / you give the money / to the clerk.
그리고 나서 / 당신은 돈을 준다 / 점원에게
But / on Yap Island, / it is different.
그러나 / 야프 섬에서는 / 그것은 다르다
People there / use stones / to buy things.
그곳의 사람들은 / 돌을 사용한다 / 물건을 사기 위해
Big stones are / as big as / two tall men.
큰 돌들은 ~이다 / ~만큼 큰 / 키 큰 남자 두 명
Small stones are / as small as / dinner plates.
작은 돌들은 ~이다 / ~만큼 작은 / 정찬용 접시
How do they move / such big stones?
어떻게 그들은 옮기는가 / 그렇게 큰 돌들을
Thankfully, / they don't carry / them.
고맙게도 / 그들은 들고 다니지 않는다 / 그것들을
They just / keep the stones / somewhere / and remember the owner.
그들은 단지 / 돌들을 둔다 / 어딘가에 / 그리고 주인을 기억한다

본문해석

당신이 무언가를 살 때, 당신은 "그것은 얼마인가요?"라고 묻는다.
그러고 나서 당신은 점원에게 돈을 준다.
하지만 야프 섬에서는 다르다.
그곳 사람들은 물건을 사기 위해 돌을 사용한다.
큰 돌들은 키 큰 남자 두 명만큼 크다.
작은 돌들은 정찬용 접시만큼 작다.
어떻게 그들은 그렇게 큰 돌들을 옮길까?
고맙게도, 그들은 그것들을 들고 다니지는 않는다.
그들은 단지 어딘가에 돌을 두고 그 주인을 기억한다.

정답

MAIN IDEA

how to buy things on Yap Island

Word Check

1 ⓐ　2 ⓒ　3 ⓓ　4 ⓑ

Grammar Check

1 as small as　2 as old as　3 as tall as

1 그 접시는 나의 손만큼 작다.
2 Jason은 Kevin만큼 나이가 들었다.
3 그 나무는 그 집만큼 높다.

Comprehension Check

1 c　2 c　3 c

2 큰 돌들은 키 큰 남자 두 명만큼 크고, 작은 돌들은 정찬용 접시만큼 작다.
3 야프 섬의 사람들이 큰 돌들로 물건을 살 때, 그들은 돌의 주인을 기억한다.

TRY IT

1) stones　2) big　3) yours

손님: 그 차는 얼마인가요?
점원: 그것은 돌 두 개입니다. 그 돌들은 키 큰 남자 두 명만큼 커야 합니다.
손님: 알겠어요. 제가 그것을 살게요. 내 돌들은 집 뒤에 있습니다. 이제 그것들은 당신 것입니다.

STORY 02 PP.12~15

Words to Learn

save: 저축하다　piggy bank: 돼지 저금통
piglet: 새끼 돼지　grow: 자라다　sick: 아픈

Grammar to Learn

그 새끼 돼지는 새끼 고양이보다 더 크다.
그 새끼 돼지는 새끼 고양이보다 더 나이가 들었다.

직독직해 P.13

Why do people / save money / in piggy banks?
왜 사람들은 ~하는가 / 돈을 저축하다 / 돼지 저금통에
Here is / the story.
여기에 ~이 있다 / 그 이야기가
There was / a boy / in a small town.
~이 있었다 / 한 소년 / 작은 마을에
His name was / Wilbur.
그의 이름은 ~였다 / Wilbur
One day, / he bought / a piglet.
어느 날 / 그는 샀다 / 새끼 돼지 한 마리를
It was / much smaller / than him.
그것은 ~이었다 / 훨씬 더 작은 / 그보다
But / it grew / and grew.
하지만 / 그것은 자랐다 / 그리고 자랐다
It became / much bigger / than him.
그것은 ~해졌다 / 훨씬 더 큰 / 그보다
Wilbur sold it / and saved the money / to help sick people.
Wilbur는 그것을 팔았다 / 그리고 그 돈을 저축했다 / 아픈 사람들을 돕기 위해
People wanted / to be / as kind as Wilbur.
사람들은 원했다 / 되기를 / Wilbur만큼 친절한
They made piggy banks / and saved money / like he did.
그들은 돼지 저금통을 만들었다 / 그리고 돈을 저축했다 / 그가 했던 것처럼

본문해석

왜 사람들은 돼지 저금통에 돈을 저축할까?
여기 그 이야기가 있다.
작은 마을에 한 소년이 있었다. 그의 이름은 Wilbur이다.
어느 날, 그가 새끼 돼지 한 마리를 샀다.
그것은 그보다 훨씬 더 작았다.
그것은 점점 자랐다.
그것은 그보다 훨씬 더 커졌다.
Wilbur는 그것을 팔아서 아픈 사람들을 돕기 위해서 돈을 저축했다.
사람들은 Wilbur만큼 친절해지고 싶었다.
그들은 돼지 저금통을 만들어서 그가 했던 것처럼 돈을 저축했다.

정답

MAIN IDEA

the first piggy bank

Word Check

1 ⓓ 2 ⓐ 3 ⓑ 4 ⓒ

Grammar Check

1 smaller than 2 taller than 3 easier than

1 그 강아지는 닭보다 더 작다.
2 Tim은 Jake보다 키가 더 크다.
3 나에게 과학은 영어보다 더 쉽다.

Comprehension Check

1 a False b True c True 2 b 3 c

1 a Wilbur는 대도시에 살았다.
b Wilbur는 새끼 돼지를 샀다.
c 그 돼지는 Wilbur보다 더 커졌다.
2 Wilbur는 아픈 사람들을 돕기 위해 그의 돼지를 팔았다.
3 사람들은 Wilbur만큼 친절해지고 싶었기 때문에 저금통을 만들었다.

TRY IT

1) 3 2) 2 3) 1 4) 4

1) Wilbur는 아픈 사람들을 도왔다.
2) Wilbur는 그의 돼지를 팔아서 그 돈을 저축했다.
3) Wilbur는 새끼 돼지를 샀고, 그것은 점점 더 자랐다.
4) 사람들은 돼지 저금통을 만들어서 Wilbur처럼 돈을 저축했다.

REVIEW TEST PP.16-17

1 grow 2 stone 3 owner 4 piglet 5 thankfully 6 Sick 7 piggy pank 8 carry 9 saved 10 clerk 11 hotter than 12 as long as 13 b 14 a False b False

1 grow: 자라다
2 stone: 돌
3 owner: 주인
4 piglet: 새끼 돼지
5 thankfully: 고맙게도
6 아픈 사람들은 병원에 간다.
7 지호는 돼지 저금통에 동전을 넣었다.
8 나는 나의 가방 안에 책 몇 권을 넣고 다닌다.
9 Dan은 돈을 저축해서 새 셔츠를 샀다.
10 나는 가게에서 점원에게 돈을 주었다.

11 오늘은 어제보다 더 덥다.
12 Ally의 머리는 Lisa의 머리만큼 길다.
14 a 그들은 물건들을 사기 위해 항상 돌들을 들고 다닌다.
b 그들이 물건을 살 때 돌들의 크기는 항상 같다.

UNIT 02 ENVIRONMENT

STORY 01 PP.20~23

Words to Learn

climb: 오르다 heavy: 무거운 oxygen bottle: 산소통
among: ~ 중에서 light: 가벼운 trash: 쓰레기

Grammar to Learn

Everest는 셋 중에 가장 높은 건물이다.
Halla는 셋 중에 가장 낮은 건물이다.

직독직해 P.21

Mt. Everest is / the highest mountain / in the world.
에베레스트 산은 ~이다 / 가장 높은 산 / 세계에서
Many people / try / to climb it.
많은 사람들이 / 노력한다 / 그것을 오르려고
When / they go up, / climbers' bags / are heavy / with a lot of things / — oxygen bottles, tents, / and other things.
~할 때 / 그들이 올라가다 / 등산객들의 가방은 / 무겁다 / 많은 것들로 / 산소통, 텐트 / 그리고 다른 것들
Oxygen bottles are / the heaviest things /among them.
산소통들은 ~이다 / 가장 무거운 것들 / 그것들 중에서
These heavy things / make / climbing harder.
이 무거운 것들은 / 만든다 / 등산을 더욱 어렵게
So / after / the climbers / use things, / they leave them / on Mt. Everest.
그래서 / ~후에 / 등산객들이 / 물건들을 사용하다 / 그들은 그것들을 남겨둔다 / 에베레스트 산에
This makes / their bags / lighter.
이것은 만든다 / 그들의 가방을 / 더 가볍게
The mountain is / still beautiful.
그 산은 ~이다 / 여전히 아름다운
But / there is / so much trash!
그러나 / ~이 있다 / 쓰레기가 너무 많이

본문해석

에베레스트 산은 세계에서 가장 높은 산이다.
많은 사람들은 그것을 오르려고 노력한다.
등산객들이 올라갈 때, 그들의 가방은 산소통과 텐트, 다른 물건들 같은 많은 것들로 무겁다.
산소통은 그것들 중 가장 무거운 것이다.

이 무거운 물건들은 등반을 더 힘들게 만든다.
그래서 등산객들은 물건을 사용한 후에 그것들을 에베레스트 산에 두고 온다.
이것은 그들의 가방을 더 가볍게 만든다.
그 산은 여전히 아름답다
하지만 쓰레기가 너무 많이 있다!

정답

MAIN IDEA

trash on Mt. Everest

Word Check

1 ⓒ 2 ⓐ 3 ⓑ 4 ⓓ

Grammar Check

1 the heaviest 2 the hottest
3 the most expensive

1 Jim은 30kg이다. Ron은 35kg이다. Alex는 38kg이다. Alex는 세 명 중 가장 무거운 소년이다.
2 대구는 32도이다. 서울은 28도이다. 속초는 25도이다. 대구는 세 곳 중 가장 더운 도시이다.
3 빨간색 가방은 30달러이다. 초록색 가방은 50달러이다. 노란색 가방은 38달러이다.
초록색 가방은 세 개 중에 가장 비싼 가방이다.

Comprehension Check

1 a 2 c 3 a

1 에베레스트 산은 세계에서 가장 높은 산이다.
2 등반객들이 에베레스트 산을 올라갈 때, 그들의 가방은 많은 물건들로 인해 무겁다.

TRY IT

1) highest 2) climb 3) trash

Nick : 무슨 일 있니? 너 화가 나 보여.
Katie: 나는 에베레스트 산에 대한 이야기를 읽었어.
Nick : 에베레스트 산? 그것은 세계에서 가장 높은 산이지?
Katie: 맞아. 매년 많은 사람들이 그곳에 올라.
슬프게도, 그들은 에베레스트 산에 그들의 쓰레기를 두고 와.
Nick : 그건 좋지 않아.

STORY 02 PP.24~27

Words to Learn

scientist: 과학자 cow: 소 hurt: 다치게 하다
fart: 방귀를 뀌다 burp: 트림하다

Grammar to Learn

그 뉴스는 매우 재미있다.
(그 뉴스는) 정말 재미있구나!
(그것은) 정말 재미있는 뉴스이구나!

직독직해 P.25

Jay : How funny / this news is! / You won't believe it!
정말 재미있구나 / 이 뉴스는 / 당신은 이것을 믿지 않을 것이다
Ann: What's going on?
무슨 일이야
Jay : Scientists say that / cows / are hurting / the Earth / when / they fart and burp.
과학자들이 ~라고 말한다 / 소들이 / 해치고 있다 / 지구를 / ~할 때 / 그들이 방귀 뀌고 트림하다
Ann: You're joking!
너 농담하는 거지
Jay : No, it's true. / A kind of gas / comes out / when / they fart and burp. / That gas / is making / the air / too hot.
아니, 그것은 사실이다 / 일종의 가스가 / 나온다 / ~할 때 / 그들이 방귀를 뀌고 트림하다 / 그 가스가 / 만들고 있다 / 공기를 / 너무 뜨겁게
Ann: How interesting!
정말 흥미롭구나
Jay : Yes. / Scientists say / that one cow makes / about 280 liters / of this gas / a day.
맞다 / 과학자들이 말하길 / 소 한 마리가 만든다 / 약 280리터 / 이 가스의 / 하루에
Ann: That's / a lot! / What surprising news!
그것은 ~이다 / 많은 / 놀라운 소식이구나

본문해석

Jay : 이 뉴스는 정말 재미있구나! 너는 이것을 믿지 않을 거야!
Ann: 무슨 일이야?
Jay : 과학자들이 말하길, 소들이 방귀를 뀌고 트림할 때 그들이 지구를 해치고 있대.
Ann: 너 농담하는 거지!
Jay : 아니야, 사실이야. 그것들이 방귀를 뀌거나 트림할 때 일종의 가스가 나온대. 그 가스가 공기를 아주 뜨겁게 만들고 있대.

Ann: 정말 흥미롭구나!
Jay : 맞아. 과학자들은 소 한 마리가 하루에 약 280리터의 가스를 만든다고 말해.
Ann: 그거 많구나! 정말 놀라운 소식이구나!

정답

MAIN IDEA

Cows Hurt the Earth

Word Check

1 ⓒ 2 ⓑ 3 ⓓ 4 ⓐ

Grammar Check

1 a cute cat (it is) 2 exciting the game is

1 그것은 정말 귀여운 고양이구나!
2 그 경기는 정말 흥미진진하구나!

Comprehension Check

1 c 2 a 3 b

1 소들은 방귀를 뀌고 트림을 할 때 지구를 해친다.
2 소들이 내뿜는 가스는 공기를 아주 뜨겁게 만든다.
3 한 마리의 소는 매일 약 280리터의 가스를 만든다.

TRY IT

Sample (Answer)
1) we drive a car 2) we drop trash on the street
3) we don't recycle the trash

우리는 ~할 때 지구를 해친다.
우리는 자동차를 운전한다
우리는 쓰레기를 길거리에 버린다
우리는 쓰레기를 재활용하지 않는다

REVIEW TEST PP.28~29

1 among 2 cow 3 burp 4 light 5 scientist
6 fart 7 climb 8 trash 9 heavy 10 hurt
11 the tallest student 12 dirty the floor is
13 beautiful pictures they are 14 How
15 a False b False

1 among: ~가운데
2 cow: 소
3 burp: 트림하다
4 light: 가벼운
5 scientist: 과학자
6 방에서 방귀를 뀌지 말아라. 그것은 나쁜 냄새가 난다.
7 그는 높은 산에 오르는 것을 좋아한다.
8 공원에 그 어떤 쓰레기도 남기지 말아라.
9 나는 가방에 많은 책들을 넣었다. 그 가방은 무겁다.
10 너무 많은 차들은 지구를 해친다.
11 Bill은 그의 반에서 가장 키가 큰 학생이다.
12 바닥이 정말 더럽구나!
13 그것들은 정말 아름다운 그림들이구나!
15 a 소들은 방귀를 뀔 때와 트림할 때 공기를 아주 차갑게 만든다.
b 한 마리의 소는 매달 280리터의 가스를 만든다.

머리 식히는 영어 퍼즐

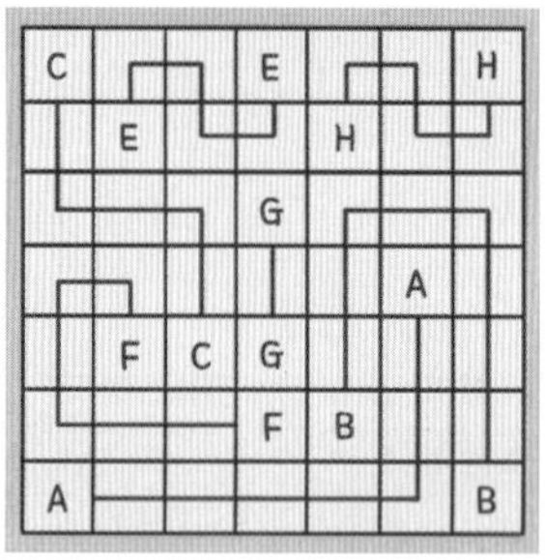

UNIT 03 MY OPINION

STORY 01 PP.32~35

Words to Learn

hallway: 복도 enter: 들어가다 behave: 행동하다
record: 녹화하다 uncomfortable: 불편한

Grammar to Learn

그 원피스는 근사해 보인다.
그 꽃은 좋은 향기가 난다.
그 피자는 맛있다.

직독직해 P.33

Many schools / have CCTV / in their hallways and classrooms.
많은 학교들은 / CCTV를 가지고 있다 / 그들의 복도와 교실 안에
But / do schools need / CCTV?
그러나 / 학교들이 필요한가 / CCTV가
First, / students can / feel safe / in school.
첫째 / 학생들은 ~할 수 있다 / 안전하다고 느끼다 / 학교에서
Bad people can't /enter the school.
나쁜 사람들은 ~할 수 없다 / 학교에 들어오다
Second, / students will not / behave badly.
둘째 / 학생들은 ~하지 않을 것이다 / 나쁘게 행동하다
They know / that CCTV can record / all their actions.
그들은 안다 / CCTV가 녹화할 수 있다는 것 / 모든 그들의 행동을
First, / teachers and students can / feel uncomfortable.
첫째 / 선생님들과 학생들은 ~할 수 있다 / 불편하게 느끼다
CCTV / is always watching / them.
CCTV가 / 항상 보고 있다 / 그들을
Second, / CCTV can't watch / every place in school.
둘째 / CCTV는 볼 수 없다 / 학교 안에 모든 장소를
Bad things / may still happen / there.
나쁜 일들은 / 계속 일어날지도 모른다 / 그 곳에서

본문해석

많은 학교의 복도와 교실에 CCTV가 있다.
하지만 학교에 CCTV가 필요한가?
그렇다:
첫째, 학생들은 학교에서 안전하다고 느낄 수 있다.
나쁜 사람들은 학교에 들어올 수 없다.
둘째, 학생들은 나쁘게 행동하지 않을 것이다.
그들은 CCTV가 그들의 모든 행동을 녹화할 수 있다는 것을 안다.
그렇지 않다:
첫째, 선생님들과 학생들은 불편하게 느낄 수 있다.
CCTV는 항상 그들을 보고 있다.
둘째, CCTV는 학교 안의 모든 장소를 볼 수는 없다.
나쁜 일들은 그곳에서 계속 일어날지도 모른다.

정답

MAIN IDEA

CCTV in school

Word Check

1 ⓒ 2 ⓑ 3 ⓐ 4 ⓓ

Grammar Check

1 soft 2 comfortable 3 good 4 interesting
5 delicious

1 그 빵은 부드럽게 느껴진다.
2 그 새 의자는 편안해 보인다.
3 그 비누는 좋은 냄새가 난다.
4 그 아이디어는 재미있게 들린다.
5 그 피자는 맛있다.

Comprehension Check

1 a, c 2 c 3 b

2 몇몇 사람들은 학교에 CCTV를 원하지 않는데 그들이 불편하게 느끼기 때문이다.
3 CCTV는 학교 모든 곳을 볼 수 없어서 나쁜 일들은 그곳에서 일어날 수 있다.

TRY IT

Sample (Answer)
YES: 학생과 교사의 안전을 지킬 수 있다.
NO: 사생활 없이 감시를 당한다고 느껴진다.

학교에 CCTV가 필요한가요?

STORY 02 PP.36~39

Words to Learn

learn: 배우다 draw: 그리다 outside: 밖에(서)
lake: 호수 nature: 자연 miss: 그리워하

Grammar to Learn

나는 항상 아침식사를 한다.
나는 절대 아침식사를 거르지 않는다.
나는 보통 밤에 책을 읽는다.
나는 때때로 밤에 TV를 본다.

직독직해 P.37

Usually, / students study / at school.
보통 / 학생들은 공부한다 / 학교에서
But / John never goes / to school.
그러나 / John은 절대 가지 않는다 / 학교에
He always learns / at home and other places.
그는 항상 배운다 / 집과 다른 장소에서
He likes / to draw / outside.
그는 좋아한다 / 그림 그리는 것을 / 밖에서
His parents often / take him / to mountains and lakes.
그의 부모님은 자주 / 그를 데리고 간다 / 산과 호수에
He draws / plants and animals / there.
그는 그린다 / 식물들과 동물들을 / 그곳에서
He goes / to the library / to read about nature.
그는 간다 / 도서관에 / 자연에 대해 읽기 위해
He likes / to visit art museums / and look at paintings.
그는 좋아한다 / 미술관을 방문하는 것을 / 그리고 그림을 보는 것을
He sometimes / misses / his friends.
그는 가끔 / 그립다 / 그의 친구들이
But he thinks / homeschooling has / many good points.
그러나 그는 생각한다 / 홈스쿨링이 가지고 있다 / 많은 장점을

본문해석

보통 학생들은 학교에서 공부한다.
하지만 John은 학교에 절대로 가지 않는다.
그는 항상 집과 다른 장소에서 배운다.
그는 밖에서 그림 그리는 것을 좋아한다.
그의 부모님은 산과 호수에 그를 자주 데리고 가신다.
그는 그곳에서 식물과 동물을 그린다.
그는 자연에 대해 읽기 위해 도서관에 간다.
그는 미술관을 방문하여 그림을 보는 것을 좋아한다.
그는 가끔씩 그의 친구들이 그립다.
하지만 그는 홈스쿨링이 많은 장점이 있다고 생각한다.

정답

MAIN IDEA

John's homeschooling

Word Check

1 ⓓ 2 ⓑ 3 ⓐ 4 ⓒ

Grammar Check

1 always 2 sometimes 3 often

1 나는 매일 늦게 일어난다. / 나는 항상 늦게 일어난다.
2 Ron은 일주일에 두 번 아침을 먹는다. / Ron은 때때로 아침을 먹는다.
3 어렸을 때 나는 많이 아팠다. / 어렸을 때 나는 자주 아팠다.

Comprehension Check

1 a 2 c 3 b, c

1 John의 부모님은 그를 산과 호수에 자주 데리고 간다.
2 John은 자연에 대해 읽기 위해 도서관에 간다.
3 John은 밖에서 그림을 그리는 것[미술관을 방문하는 것]을 좋아한다.

TRY IT

Sample (Answer)
Q1 자신의 적성과 흥미에 맞는 공부를 할 수 있다.
Q2 친구를 사귀기가 어렵다.

홈스쿨링의 장점은 무엇인가요?
홈스쿨링의 단점은 무엇인가요?

REVIEW TEST PP.40~41

1 enter 2 hallway 3 uncomfortable
4 nature 5 draw 6 outside 7 recorded
8 missed 9 learn 10 lake 11 feel tired
12 sounded sad 13 looked strong 14 b
15 a True b False

1 enter: 들어가다
2 hallway: 복도
3 uncomfortable: 불편한

4 nature: 자연
5 draw: 그리다
6 비가 많이 오고 있다. 밖에 나가지 마라
7 Ann은 아들의 춤을 녹화했다.
8 민호는 그의 가족을 매우 그리워했다.
9 Cindy는 영어 배우는 것을 좋아한다.
10 그 소년들은 호수에서 수영하고 있다.
11 나는 어젯밤에 충분한 잠을 자지 못했다. 나는 피곤함을 느낀다.
12 어제 그 음악은 슬프게 들렸다. 사람들은 많이 울었다.
13 그 남자는 무거운 상자를 들고 있었다. 그는 힘이 세 보였다.
15 a John은 집과 다른 장소에서 배운다.
b John은 그의 친구들을 그리워하지 않는다.

UNIT 04 SHOPPING

STORY 01 PP. 44~47

Words to Learn

cart: 카트, 손수레 way: 방법 reason 이유
full: 가득 찬 push: 밀다 secret: 비밀

Grammar to Learn

사람들은 그를 Hulk라고 불렀다.
악당은 그를 화나게 만들었다.
Hulk는 악당을 쓰러지게 만들었다.

직독직해 P. 45

Malls try / to make people buy / more things.
쇼핑몰들은 노력한다 / 사람들이 사게 만들려고 / 더 많은 물건들을
Carts are / one way / of doing this.
카트들이 ~이다 / 한 방법 / 이렇게 하는 것의
Malls make them / big and heavy / for special reasons.
쇼핑몰들은 그것들을 만든다 / 크고 무겁게 / 특별한 이유들로
First, / if / a cart is not full, / people feel / they buy little.
첫째 / 만약 ~한다면 / 카트가 꽉 차지 않는다 / 사람들은 느낀다 / 그들이 조금 산다고
So / they put / more things / into it.
그래서 / 그들은 넣는다 / 더 많은 물건들을 / 그것 안에
Second, / people can't push / heavy carts / fast.
둘째 / 사람들은 밀 수 없다 / 무거운 카트를 / 빨리
They move / slowly / and buy / more things.
그들은 움직인다 / 천천히 / 그리고 산다 / 더 많은 물건들을
Big and heavy / carts are / the big secret / for malls.
크고 무거운 / 카트들은 ~이다 / 큰 비밀 / 쇼핑몰들에게

본문해석

쇼핑몰은 사람들이 더 많은 물건을 사게 만들려고 노력한다.
카트는 이렇게 하는 것의 한 방법이다.
쇼핑몰은 특별한 이유들로 그것들을 크고 무겁게 만든다.
첫 번째, 만약 카트가 가득 차지 않았다면 사람들은 그들이 조금 산다고 느낀다.
그래서 그들은 그것 안에 더 많은 물건들을 넣는다.
두 번째, 사람들은 무거운 카트를 빠르게 밀 수 없다.
그들은 천천히 움직이며 더 많은 물건들을 산다.
크고 무거운 카트는 쇼핑몰의 큰 비밀이다.

정답

MAIN IDEA

the secret of carts in the mall

Word Check

1 ⓒ 2 ⓐ 3 ⓑ 4 ⓓ

Grammar Check

1 sad 2 laugh 3 famous 4 delicious 5 do

1 그 음악은 나를 슬프게 만들었다.
2 Jim은 항상 사람들을 웃게 만든다.
3 그 책은 그를 유명하게 만들었다.
4 이 소스는 어떤 음식이라도 맛있게 만들 수 있다.
5 나의 선생님은 우리가 많은 숙제를 하게 만들었다

Comprehension Check

1 c 2 c 3 b

1 쇼핑몰은 사람들이 더 많은 물건을 사게 만들기 위해 노력한다.
2 만약 카트가 가득 차지 않는다면, 사람들은 그것 안에 더 많은 물건을 넣는다.
3 쇼핑몰이 카트를 무겁게 만들어서 사람들이 카트를 빨리 움직일 수 없다.

TRY IT

1) little 2) slowly 3) more

쇼핑몰은 카트를 크게 만든다. ➡ 사람들은 적게 산다고 느낀다.
쇼핑몰은 카트를 무겁게 만든다. ➡ 사람들은 카트를 천천히 민다.
⬇
사람들은 더 많은 물건을 산다.

STORY 02 PP.48~51

Words to Learn

look for: 찾다 flavor: 맛 price: 가격
be made from: ~로 만들어지다 cheaply: 싸게,저렴하게
fair: 공정한

Grammar to Learn

더울 때, 에어컨을 켜라.
만약 창문이 열려있다면, 그것을 닫아라.
에어컨이 켜져 있기 때문에 곧 시원해질 것이다.

직독직해 P.49

When / you buy chocolate, / what do you / look for?
~할 때 / 당신이 초콜릿을 산다 / 당신은 무엇을 하는가 / 찾다
Flavor? / The price?
맛 / 가격
Why don't you / look for / the Fair Trade sign?
~하는 것은 어떤가 / 찾다 / 공정무역 표시를
Chocolate / is made from / cocoa beans.
초콜릿은 / ~로 만들어진다 / 카카오 열매
Farmers work / long hours.
농부들은 일한다 / 긴 시간
But big companies buy / cocoa beans / from them / too cheaply.
그러나 큰 기업들은 산다 / 카카오 열매를 / 그들로부터 / 너무 싸게
Because / some think / this is not / fair, / a new company / started.
~ 때문에 / 어떤 사람들이 생각한다 / 이것이 ~가 아니다 / 공평한 / 한 새로운 회사가 / 설립되었다
It buys / cocoa beans / at a fair price.
그것은 산다 / 카카오 열매를 / 공정한 가격에
The farmers get / more money.
농부들은 얻는다 / 더 많은 돈을
If / you buy / chocolate / with the Fair Trade sign, / you can help / make the world / better.
만약 ~한다면 / 당신이 산다 / 초콜릿을 / 공정무역 표시가 있는 / 당신은 도울 수 있다 / 세상을 만드는 것을 / 더 좋게

본문해석

당신은 초콜릿을 살 때, 무엇을 찾아봅니까?
맛? 가격?
공정무역 표시를 찾아보는 것이 어떻습니까?
초콜릿은 카카오 열매로 만들어집니다.
농부들은 오랜 시간 동안 일합니다.
하지만 대기업들은 그들로부터 카카오 열매를 너무 싸게 삽니다.
몇몇 사람들이 이것이 불공정하다고 생각해서, 새로운 회사가 설립되었습니다.
그것은 공정한 가격으로 카카오 열매를 삽니다.
농부들은 더 많은 돈을 받습니다.
만약 당신이 공정무역 표시가 붙은 초콜릿을 산다면, 당신은 세상을 더 좋게 만드는 것을 도울 수 있습니다.

정답

MAIN IDEA

Fair Trade chocolate

Word Check

1 ⓒ 2 ⓐ 3 ⓓ 4 ⓑ

Grammar Check

1 when 2 because 3 when 4 If 5 because
6 If

1 나는 어렸을 때 미국에서 살았다.
2 어젯밤 Tom은 아파서 일찍 잠자리에 들었다.
3 Joy가 나에게 전화를 했을 때 나는 바빴다.
4 질문이 있다면 저에게 물어봐 주세요.
5 Susan은 강아지를 잃어버려서 슬프다.
6 내가 민수를 만난다면 나는 매우 기쁠 것이다.

Comprehension Check

1 b 2 a 3 c

1 초콜릿은 카카오 열매로 만든다.
2 농부들은 오랜 시간 일하지만 그들은 대기업으로부터 적은 돈을 받는다.
3 공정무역 표시가 있는 초콜릿을 사면, 우리는 세상을 더 좋게 만드는 것을 도울 수 있다.

TRY IT

1) long 2) cheaply 3) fair 4) more

문제점: 농부들은 오랜 시간 동안 일한다. 대기업들은 카카오 열매를 너무 싸게 산다.
해결책: 공정무역
결과: 새로운 회사는 공정한 가격에 카카오 열매를 산다. 농부들은 더 많은 돈을 번다.

REVIEW TEST PP. 52-53

1 price 2 push 3 reason 4 fair 5 cart
6 full 7 secret 8 flavor 9 is made from
10 cheaply 11 Because 12 When
13 a False b True 14 a

1 price: 가격
2 push: 밀다
3 reason: 이유
4 fair: 공정한
5 cart: 카트, 손수레
6 그 방은 장난감으로 가득 차 있다.
7 Lily는 그녀의 비밀을 말하는 것을 원하지 않는다.
8 내가 가장 좋아하는 아이스크림 맛은 초콜릿이다.
9 치즈는 우유로 만들어진다.
10 나는 그 자동차를 저렴하게 샀다.
11 내일 시험이 있기 때문에, 나는 공부를 해야 한다.
12 당신은 생선을 살 때, 그것들의 눈 색깔을 확인해라.
13 a 대기업들은 공정한 가격에 카카오 열매를 산다.
b 새로운 회사가 설립된 후, 농부들은 더 많은 돈을 번다.

UNIT 05 GOOD INVENTIONS

STORY 01 PP.56~59

Words to Learn

normal: 평범한　press: 누르다　remote control: 리모컨
pick up: 집어 들다　technology: 기술
convenient: 편리한

Grammar to Learn

그 음식점은 근사해 보인다.
그것은 비행기처럼 보인다.
이 빵은 맛있다.
그것은 피자 같은 맛이 난다.

직독직해 P.57

A new shoe store / opened.
새로운 신발 가게가 / 문을 열었다
It looks / normal, / but it is / different.
그것은 ~해 보인다 / 평범한 / 하지만 그것은 ~이다 / 다른
Usually / people use / a ladder / to reach the shoes / on the top shelves.
대개 / 사람들은 사용한다 / 사다리를 / 신발에 닿기 위해 / 꼭대기 선반 위의
But here, / drones carry / the shoes.
하지만 여기에서는 / 드론이 나른다 / 신발을
A clerk presses / a button / on a remote control.
점원은 누른다 / 버튼을 / 리모컨 위의
Then, / a drone flies / to pick up / the shoes.
그러면 / 드론이 난다 / 집기 위해 / 신발을
They look like / airplanes.
그것들은 ~같이 보인다 / 비행기
But / there is / no pilot.
하지만 / ~이 있다 / 조종사가 없는
Technology / makes shopping / more convenient.
기술은 / 쇼핑을 만든다 / 더 편리하게

본문해석

새로운 신발 가게가 문을 열었다.
이 가게는 평범해 보이지만, 그곳은 다르다.
보통 사람들은 꼭대기 선반에 있는 신발에 닿기 위해 사다리를 사용한다.
그러나 여기서는 드론이 신발을 나른다.
점원은 리모컨의 버튼을 누른다.
그러면 드론이 신발을 집으러 날아간다.
그것들은 비행기같이 보인다. 하지만 조종사가 없다.
기술이 쇼핑을 더 편리하게 만든다.

정답

MAIN IDEA

The Shoe Store with Drones

Word Check

1 ⓑ　2 ⓒ　3 ⓐ　4 ⓓ

Grammar Check

1 look　2 look like　3 tastes like　4 tastes
5 smells like

1 그 신발은 편안해 보인다.
2 그 로봇들은 사람 같아 보인다.
3 그 수프는 카레 같은 맛이 난다.
4 그 차는 맛이 좋다.
5 그 초는 장미 같은 냄새가 난다.

Comprehension Check

1 b　2 c　3 c

1 드론은 신발을 집으러 날아간다.
2 드론은 비행기 같아 보인다.
3 그들은 리모컨으로 드론을 조종한다.

TRY IT

1) ladders　2) press the button　3) convenient

스마트 신발 가게
우리 신발 가게는 다릅니다.
우리는 사다리가 없습니다.
그러나 우리는 꼭대기 선반에 있는 신발에 닿을 수 있죠.
그저 리모컨에 있는 버튼을 누르기만 하세요!
그러면 드론이 당신의 신발을 가져옵니다.
우리 가게에서 쇼핑하는 것은 편리합니다.

STORY 02 PP.60~63

Words to Learn

across: 가로질러, 맞은편에　invent: 발명하다

traffic light: 신호등 side: 쪽 copy: 따라 하다

Grammar to Learn

나는 영화 보기를 즐긴다.
나는 숙제하는 것을 끝냈다.
나는 계속 팝콘을 먹었다.
나는 중국어를 배우기를 원한다.
나는 중국어를 열심히 공부하기로 결심했다.
나는 책 몇 권을 사야 했다.

직독직해 P.61

Some people / walk across the road / at red lights.
몇몇 사람들은 / 길을 건넌다 / 빨간불에
They are busy / or / simply don't want to wait.
그들은 바쁘다 / 혹은 / 단순히 기다리고 싶지 않다
But / it is / dangerous.
하지만 / 그것은 ~이다 / 위험한
One company wanted / to make waiting / fun.
한 회사는 원했다 / 기다림을 만들기를 / 재미있게
So / it invented / a dancing traffic light!
그래서 / 그것은 발명했다 / 춤추는 신호등을
On one side / of the road, / a person dances / in a special box.
한 편에서는 / 길의 / 한 사람이 춤춘다 / 특별한 상자 안에서
The red light copies / the dance.
빨간불은 따라 한다 / 그 춤을
Across the road, / people enjoy / watching the dancing light.
길 맞은편에서 / 사람들은 즐긴다 / 춤추는 신호등을 보는 것을
They enjoy / waiting!
그들은 즐긴다 / 기다리는 것을
This great idea / made the city / safer.
이 훌륭한 아이디어가 / 도시를 만들었다 / 더 안전하게

본문해석

어떤 사람들은 빨간불에 길을 건넌다.
그들은 바쁘거나 단순히 기다리고 싶어하지 않는다.
하지만 그것은 위험하다.
한 회사는 기다림을 재미있게 만들고 싶어했다.
그래서 춤추는 신호등을 발명했다!
길의 한 쪽에서는, 한 사람이 특별한 상자 안에서 춤을 춘다.
빨간불이 그 춤을 따라 한다.
길 맞은편에서, 사람들이 춤추는 신호등을 보는 것을 즐긴다.
그들은 기다리는 것을 즐거워한다!
이 훌륭한 아이디어가 도시를 더 안전하게 만들었다.

정답

MAIN IDEA

The Dancing Traffic Light

Word Check

1 ⓓ 2 ⓒ 3 ⓑ 4 ⓐ

Grammar Check

1 to know 2 dancing 3 reading 4 to see
5 to do

1 나는 그것에 대해 알고 싶다.
2 Jake는 사람들 앞에서 춤추는 것을 즐긴다.
3 현아는 책 읽기를 끝냈다.
4 나는 곧 당신을 봐야 한다.
5 그들은 그들의 숙제를 먼저 하기로 결정했다.

Comprehension Check

1 a 2 c 3 a

1 한 회사가 신호등 기다리는 것을 재미있게 만들고 싶어했다.
2 빨간불은 특별한 상자 속 사람의 춤을 따라 한다.
3 춤추는 신호등은 도시를 더 안전하게 만들었다.

TRY IT

1) red lights 2) dancing 3) waiting

문제점: 사람들은 빨간불에 길을 건넌다.
해결책: 한 회사가 춤추는 신호등을 발명했다.
결과: 이제 사람들은 기다리는 것을 즐긴다. 도시는 더 안전하다.

REVIEW TEST PP.66-67

1 copy 2 across 3 press 4 invent
5 convenient 6 traffic light 7 normal
8 remote control 9 Technology 10 picked up 11 looks like 12 to eat 13 c
14 a False b False c False

1 copy: 따라 하다
2 across: 가로질러, 맞은편에
3 press: 누르다
4 invent: 발명하다
5 convenient: 편리한

6 길을 건널 때 신호등을 봐라.
7 이것은 평범해 보이지만 많은 특별한 용도를 가지고 있다.
8 나는 리모컨으로 TV를 켰다.
9 기술은 우리의 삶을 편리하게 만들어 준다.
10 나는 길 위의 쓰레기를 주웠다.
11 그는 다른 사람같아 보인다.
12 James는 아이스크림을 먹고 싶어한다.
14 **a** 이 가게는 다른 가게들과 달라 보인다.
b 사람들은 이 신발 가게에서 사다리를 사용한다.
c 점원들이 신발을 집기 위해 날아 간다.

UNIT 06 TECHNOLOGY

STORY 01 PP.68~71

Words to Learn

sign: 표지판 painting: 그림 rule: 규칙
visitor: 방문객 blind: 시각 장애가 있는

Grammar to Learn

그녀는 이 미술관을 좋아할지도 모른다.
그는 이 미술관을 좋아하지 않을지도 모른다.
이 그림들은 만져도 된다.
여기서 사진을 찍으면 안 된다.

직독직해 P.69

You may often see / this sign / in art museums:
당신은 종종 볼지도 모른다 / 이 표지판을 / 미술관에서
"Don't touch / the paintings."
만지지 마라 / 그림들을
But / the rule is different / in this 3D museum.
하지만 / 규칙이 다르다 / 이 3D 미술관에서는
Visitors / may touch / the paintings!
방문객들은 / 만져도 된다 / 그림들을
3D printers / made them.
3D 프린터가 / 그것들을 만들었다
People / may touch / Mona Lisa's face.
사람들은 / 만져도 된다 / 모나리자의 얼굴을
They can feel / her smile / by touch.
그들은 느낄 수 있다 / 그녀의 미소를 / 손으로 만져서
This is / good news / for blind people.
이것은 ~이다 / 좋은 소식 / 시각 장애인들에게
Until now, / they could not enjoy / the paintings.
지금까지 / 그들은 즐길 수 없었다 / 그림들을
3D technology / brings them / happiness.
3D 기술은 / 그들에게 가져다 준다 / 행복을
But / the paintings / may not be / so clean!
하지만 / 그림들은 / ~지 않을지도 모른다 / 그렇게 깨끗한

본문해석

당신은 미술관에서 종종 이런 표지판을 볼 지도 모른다.
'그림을 만지지 마시오!'
그러나 이 3D 미술관에서는 규칙이 다르다.
방문객들은 그림을 만져도 된다!
3D 프린터가 그것들을 만들었다.
사람들은 모나리자의 얼굴을 만져도 된다.
그들은 손으로 만져서 그녀의 웃음을 느낄 수 있다.

이것은 시각 장애인들에게 좋은 소식이다.
지금까지, 그들은 그림을 즐길 수 없었다.
3D 기술은 그들에게 행복을 가져다준다.
그러나 그림들은 그다지 깨끗하지 않을지도 모른다!

정답

MAIN IDEA

a 3D museum

Word Check

1 ⓑ 2 ⓓ 3 ⓐ 4 ⓒ

Grammar Check

1 ~해도 좋다 2 ~할지도 모른다 3 ~하면 안 된다
4 ~할지도 모른다 5 ~해도 좋다

1 당신은 내 스마트폰을 사용해도 좋다.
2 그녀는 이 액션 영화를 좋아할지도 모른다.
3 당신은 TV를 너무 많이 봐서는 안 된다.
4 그들은 아마도 중학생일지도 모른다.
5 이 그림 만져도 되나요?

Comprehension Check

1 a 2 c 3 c

1 3D 미술관에서는 규칙이 다른 미술관의 규칙과 다르다.
2 3D 기술은 시각 장애인들이 그림을 즐기도록 도와준다.
3 3D 미술관의 그림들은 깨끗하지 않을지도 모른다.

TRY IT

1) may 2) can 3) may not 4) can

3D 미술관에서
사람들은 그림을 만져도 된다.
사람들은 그림을 느낄 수 있다.
다른 미술관에서
사람들은 그림을 만지면 안 된다.
사람들은 그림을 볼 수 있다.

STORY 02 PP.72~75

Words to Learn

turn off: (전원을) 끄다 connect: 연결하다
machine: 기계 control: 조종하다 break down: 고장 나다

Grammar to Learn

나는 선생님이다.
그는 요리사이다.
그들은 무용수이다.
나는 지금 가르치고 있다.
그는 지금 요리하고 있다.
그들은 지금 춤추고 있다.

직독직해 P.73

Jenny is eating / at a restaurant.
Jenny는 먹고 있다 / 식당에서
Her smartphone / rings.
그녀의 스마트폰이 / 울린다
It is / a message / from her home.
그것은 ~이다 / 메시지 / 그녀의 집으로부터
It says, / "You left / your heating on."
그것은 ~라고 쓰여있다 / 당신은 남겨두었다 / 난방을 킨
She uses / her phone / to turn off / her heating.
그녀는 사용한다 / 휴대전화를 / 끄기 위해 / 그녀의 난방을
The Internet / is connecting / all machines / together.
인터넷은 / 연결하고 있다 / 모든 기계를 / 함께
People call this / the Internet of Things(IoT).
사람들은 이것을 부른다 / 사물 인터넷이라고
With this, / you can / control things / with your smartphone.
이것을 가지고 / 당신은 ~할 수 있다 / 사물들을 조종하다 / 당신의 스마트폰으로
It makes / our life / convenient.
이것은 만든다 / 우리의 삶을 / 편리한
But / there is / a problem.
하지만 / ~가 있다 / 문제
If / a virus attacks, / all machines / will break down.
만약 ~한다면 / 바이러스가 공격한다 / 모든 기계들은 / 고장 날 것이다

본문해석

Jenny는 식당에서 식사를 하고 있다.
그녀의 스마트폰이 울린다.
그것은 집에서 온 메시지이다.
그것에는, "난방이 켜져 있습니다"라고 쓰여 있다.
그녀는 휴대전화를 사용해 난방을 끈다.
인터넷이 모든 기계들을 함께 연결하고 있다.
사람들은 이것을 사물인터넷(IoT)이라고 부른다.
이것으로, 당신은 스마트폰을 이용해 사물들을 조종할 수 있다.
이것은 우리의 삶을 편리하게 한다. 그러나 문제가 있다.
만약 바이러스가 공격하면, 모든 기계들은 고장 날 것이다.

정답

MAIN IDEA

the Internet of Things

Word Check

1 ⓒ 2 ⓓ 3 ⓐ 4 ⓑ

Grammar Check

1 is driving 2 are studying 3 are eating

1 우리 아버지는 지금 빨간 차를 운전하고 계신다.
2 그들은 지금 중국어를 공부하고 있다.
3 내 여동생들은 지금 과일을 먹고 있다.

Comprehension Check

1 c 2 b 3 a

2 인터넷은 모든 기계들을 연결한다.
3 만약 바이러스가 공격한다면 모든 기계들은 고장 날 것이다.

TRY IT

1) control 2) convenient 3) break down

사물 인터넷
좋은 점: 당신은 스마트폰으로 기계들을 조종할 수 있다.
그것은 우리의 삶을 편리하게 해준다.
나쁜 점: 만약 바이러스가 있다면 모든 기계들은 고장 날 수 있다.

REVIEW TEST PP.76-77

1 machine 2 blind 3 painting 4 visitor
5 break down 6 Turn off 7 connects
8 rules 9 control 10 sign 11 is studying
12 is playing 13 c 14 a False b False

1 machine: 기계
2 bind: 시각 장애가 있는
3 painting: 그림
4 visitor: 방문객
5 break down: 고장 나다
6 교실에서는 전화기를 꺼라.
7 그 다리는 두 도시를 연결한다.
8 여기서 당신은 우리의 규칙을 따라야 한다.
9 나는 내 스마트폰으로 그 로봇을 조종할 수 있다.
10 벽 위의 표지판에, '만지지 마시오'라고 쓰여 있다.
11 진호는 지금 영어를 공부하고 있다.
12 소라는 지금 컴퓨터 게임을 하고 있다.
14 a Jenny는 집에서만 난방을 끌 수 있다.
b 기계들은 절대 고장 나지 않을 것이다.

UNIT 07 IN SPACE

STORY 01 PP.80~83

Words to Learn

astronaut: 우주비행사 space: 우주
float: (공중에서) 떠가다 spaceship: 우주선 tie: 묶다

Grammar to Learn

나는/당신(들)은/우리는/그들은 조심해야 한다.
그/그녀는 조심해야 한다.

직독직해 P.83

Jane is / an astronaut.
Jane은 ~이다 / 우주비행사
She sometimes travels / into space.
그녀는 때때로 여행한다 / 우주로
In space, / she needs / to eat, sleep, / and use the bathroom.
우주에서 / 그녀는 ~해야 한다 / 먹고 자다 / 그리고 화장실을 사용하다
When / she eats, / she must / be careful.
~할 때 / 그녀가 먹는다 / 그녀는 ~해야 한다 / 조심하다
If not, / her food can / float around / in the spaceship.
그렇지 않으면 / 그녀의 음식은 ~할 수 있다 / 떠다니다 / 우주선 안을
When / she sleeps, / she must tie herself / to her bed.
~할 때 / 그녀가 자다 / 그녀는 자신을 묶어야 한다 / 그녀의 침대에
She also / has to tie herself / to the toilet / in the bathroom.
그녀는 또한 / 자신을 묶어야 한다 / 변기에 / 화장실에서
It's / a little difficult, / but / she is happy.
그것은 ~이다 / 조금 어려운 / 하지만 / 그녀는 행복하다
She can see / the beautiful Earth / every day.
그녀는 볼 수 있다 / 아름다운 지구를 / 매일

본문해석

Jane은 우주비행사이다.
그녀는 가끔 우주를 여행한다.
우주에서 그녀는 먹고, 자고, 화장실을 사용해야 한다.
그녀가 먹을 때, 그녀는 조심해야 한다.
그렇지 않으면, 그녀의 음식은 우주선 안에서 떠다닐 수 있다.
그녀가 잘 때, 그녀는 자신을 침대에 묶거나 침낭에서 자야 한다.
그녀는 또한 화장실에서 자신을 변기에 묶어야 한다.
이것은 조금 힘들지만, 그녀는 행복하다.
그녀는 아름다운 지구를 매일 볼 수 있다.

정답

MAIN IDEA

Life in Space

Word Check

1 ⓒ 2 ⓑ 3 ⓐ 4 ⓓ

Grammar Check

1 must, have to 2 must, has to

1 당신은 도서관 안에서는 조용히 해야 한다.
2 그는 횡단보도에서 조심해야 한다.

Comprehension Check

1 c 2 c 3 b

1 우주에서의 생활은 어렵다.
2 우주비행사들은 잠을 잘 때 무엇을 하는가?
3 Jane은 매일 아름다운 지구를 볼 수 있어서 행복하다.

TRY IT

1) float around 2) tie 3) tie

우주에서의 생활
음식 Q: 그들은 왜 조심해서 먹는가?
A: 우주선에서는 음식이 떠다닐 수 있다.
잠 Q: 그들은 어떻게 잘 수 있는가?
A: 그들은 자신을 침대에 묶는다.
화장실 Q: 그들은 어떻게 화장실을 사용하는가?
A: 그들은 자신을 변기에 묶는다.

STORY 02 PP.84~87

Words to Learn

turn on: (전기 등을) 켜다 shoot: (총 등을) 쏘다
loud: 시끄러운 silent: 조용한
turn down: (소리 등을) 낮추다

Grammar to Learn

영화는 잘못된 것이 틀림없다.
사람들은 우주에서 특수복을 입어야 한다.
영화는 진짜일 리가 없다.
사람들은 우주에서 특수복이 없으면 살 수 없다.

직독직해 P.87

Turn on / the TV.
켜라 / TV를
It's time to watch / *Star Wars*.
볼 시간이다 / 〈스타워즈〉를
You must listen to / the sounds.
너는 틀림없이 ~를 들을 것이다 / 소리
Boom! Zap! Bam!
쿵! 휙! 탕!
Two spaceships / are shooting / at each other.
두 우주선은 / 쏘고 있다 / 서로에게
It is / very loud.
그것은 ~이다 / 매우 시끄러운
But / these sounds / cannot be real!
하지만 / 이 소리들은 / 진짜일 리 없다
Moving air makes / sound, / but there is no air / in space.
움직이는 공기가 만든다 / 소리를 / 하지만 공기가 없다 / 우주에는
That means / space is / silent.
그것은 ~을 의미한다 / 우주가 ~이다 / 고요한
The sounds / in *Star Wars* / cannot happen.
소리는 / 〈스타워즈〉에서의 / 발생할 수 없다
Next time / you watch *Star Wars*, / turn down / the volume!
다음 번 / 당신이 〈스타워즈〉를 보다 / 줄여라 / 소리를

본문해석

TV를 켜라. 〈스타워즈〉를 볼 시간이다.
당신은 틀림없이 소리를 들을 것이다.
쿵! 휙! 탕!
우주선 두 대가 서로를 향해 쏘고 있다.
그것은 매우 시끄럽다.
그러나 이 소리들은 진짜일 리가 없다!
움직이는 공기가 소리를 만들지만, 우주에는 공기가 없다.
그것은 우주가 고요하다는 것을 의미한다.
〈스타워즈〉의 소리는 일어날 수 없다.
다음에 〈스타워즈〉를 볼 때에, 소리를 줄여라!

정답

MAIN IDEA

sounds in space

Word Check

1 ⓑ 2 ⓓ 3 ⓒ 4 ⓐ

Grammar Check

1 must 2 cannot 3 cannot 4 must 5 must

1 그는 오늘 학교에 오지 않았다. 그는 아픈 것이 틀림없다.
2 그들은 자고 있다. 그들이 컴퓨터를 사용할 리가 없다.
3 그 이야기는 사실일 리가 없다. 나는 그것을 믿지 않는다!
4 그녀는 지금 TV를 보고 있음에 틀림없다. 그녀는 언제나 TV를 본다.
5 〈스타워즈〉는 매우 재미있음이 틀림없다. 모두가 그것을 좋아한다.

Comprehension Check

1 c 2 a 3 b

1 〈스타워즈〉의 시끄러운 소리는 진짜일 리가 없다.
2 움직이는 공기가 소리를 만든다.
3 우주에는 공기가 없어서 소리가 없다.

TRY IT

turn down the volume

Sue : 뭐 하고 있니?
Sam: 〈스타워즈〉 보고 있어. 그것의 소리는 매우 커!
Sue : 우주의 진짜 소리를 느끼고 싶다면, 소리를 줄여야 해.

REVIEW TEST PP.90~91

1 loud 2 tie 3 shoot 4 space 5 astronaut 6 Turn down 7 spaceship 8 silent 9 floating 10 turned on 11 cannot 12 must 13 must[has to] 14 c 15 a False b False

1 loud: 시끄러운
2 tie: 묶다
3 shoot: 쏘다
4 space: 우주
5 astronaut: 우주비행사

6 너무 시끄럽다. 볼륨을 낮춰라.
7 우주인들은 우주선 안에서 여행한다.
8 방에서 아무도 이야기하지 않는다. 그 방은 조용하다.
9 빨간 풍선이 공중에 떠다니고 있다.
10 그 방이 어두워서 나는 불을 켰다.
11 그녀는 막 점심을 먹었다. 지금 배고플 리가 없다.
12 진수는 영어를 매우 열심히 공부했다. 그는 좋은 점수를 받을 것임에 틀림없다.
13 Joe는 도서관에 있다. 그녀는 조용히 해야 한다.
15 a 우주에서 Jane은 잠을 잘 필요가 없다.
b Jane은 지구를 볼 수 없기 때문에 행복하지 않다.

UNIT 08 TRADITIONS

STORY 01 PP.92~95

Words to Learn

doll: 인형 worry: 걱정 take away: 없애 주다
pillow: 베개 disappear: 사라지다

Grammar to Learn

나는 David에게 나의 걱정들을 이야기한다.

직독직해 P.93

Lucy has / a doll.
Lucy는 가지고 있다 / 인형을
It looks sad, / but it has / a special power.
그것은 슬퍼 보인다 / 하지만 그것은 가지고 있다 / 특별한 힘을
When / she tells it / her worries, / it takes them away.
~할 때 / 그녀가 그것에게 말하다 / 그녀의 걱정들을 / 그것은 걱정을 없애 준다
It's / a traditional Mayan doll.
그것은 ~이다 / 전통적인 마야 인형
Mayan people / told dolls / their worries.
마야인들은 / 인형에게 말했다 / 그들의 걱정들을
And then / they put / the dolls / under their pillows / at night.
그러고 나서 / 그들은 넣는다 / 인형을 / 그들의 베개 밑에 / 밤에
The dolls took away / their worries.
그 인형들은 없애 주었다 / 그들의 걱정을
Lucy told / her worries / to her doll / like Mayan people did.
Lucy는 말했다 / 그녀의 걱정을 / 그녀의 인형에게 / 마야인들이 했던 것처럼
She hopes / her worries disappear / by the morning.
그녀는 바란다 / 그녀의 걱정이 사라지기를 / 아침쯤에는

본문해석

Lucy는 인형을 하나 가지고 있다.
이것은 슬퍼 보이지만, 특별한 힘을 가지고 있다.
그녀가 그것에게 걱정을 말하면, 그것은 그것들을 없애 준다.
이것은 전통적인 마야 인형이다.
마야인들은 인형에게 그들의 걱정을 말했다.

그러고 나서 그들은 밤에 인형을 그들의 베개 밑에 넣었다.
인형들은 그들의 걱정을 없애 주었다.
Lucy는 마야인들이 했던 것처럼 그녀의 걱정을 그녀의 인형에게 말했다.
그녀는 아침쯤이면 그녀의 걱정들이 사라지기를 바란다.

정답

MAIN IDEA

A Special Doll

Word Check

1 ⓑ 2 ⓓ 3 ⓐ 4 ⓒ

Grammar Check

1 tell my story to you 2 told the news to us

1 내 이야기를 너에게 말해줄게.
2 우리 선생님은 우리에게 그 소식을 말해주셨다.

Comprehension Check

1 a 2 b 3 b

2 밤에 마야인들은 전통 인형을 그들의 베개 아래에 두었다.
3 전통적인 마야 인형은 사람들의 걱정을 없애 주었다.

TRY IT

1) 2 2) 1 3) 3

Lucy에게 걱정이 있을 때, 무슨 일이 일어나는가?
1) Lucy는 인형을 베개 아래에 넣는다.
2) Lucy가 인형에게 그녀의 걱정을 말해준다.
3) 인형은 Lucy의 걱정을 없애 준다.

STORY 02 PP.96~99

Words to Learn

hang from: ~에 매달리다, ~에서 드리워지다 cliff: 절벽
hold onto: ~에 매달리다 honey: 꿀 hive: 벌집
fall: 떨어지다

Grammar to Learn

Jake의 취미는 쿠키를 굽는 것이다.
쿠키를 굽는 것은 재미있다.
그는 쿠키를 굽는 것을 좋아한다.
Katie는 쿠키를 만들고 있다.
그녀는 초콜릿 칩을 넣고 있다.

직독직해 P.97

A long rope ladder / hangs from / the top of a cliff.
긴 밧줄 사다리가 / ~에서 드리워진다 / 절벽의 꼭대기
A man / is holding onto / the ladder.
한 남자가 / ~에 매달려 있다 / 사다리
His job is / collecting honey.
그의 직업은 ~이다 / 꿀을 모으는 것
He uses / long sticks / to get the honey.
그는 사용한다 / 긴 막대들을 / 꿀을 얻기 위해
It is / the best honey / in the world.
그것은 ~이다 / 최고의 꿀 / 세계에서
But / getting the honey / is not easy / because / the hives are on a cliff.
하지만 / 꿀을 얻는 것은 / 쉽지 않다 / ~때문에 / 벌집들이 절벽에 있다
It is / very dangerous.
그것은 ~이다 / 몹시 위험한
Only / the ladder can keep / him from falling.
오직 / 사다리만이 방지할 수 있다 / 그가 떨어지는 것을
This is / a traditional job / in Nepal.
그것은 ~이다 / 전통적인 직업 / 네팔에서

본문해석

긴 밧줄 사다리가 절벽 꼭대기에서 드리워진다.
한 남자가 그 사다리에 매달려 있다.
그의 직업은 꿀을 모으는 것이다.
그는 꿀을 얻기 위해 긴 막대를 사용한다.
그것은 세계에서 가장 좋은 꿀이다.
그러나 벌집들이 절벽에 있기 때문에 꿀을 얻는 것은 쉽지 않다.
그것은 매우 위험하다.
사다리만이 그가 떨어지는 것을 방지할 수 있다.
이것은 네팔의 전통적인 직업이다.

정답

MAIN IDEA

a traditional job in Nepal

Word Check

1 ⓑ 2 ⓓ 3 ⓐ 4 ⓒ

Grammar Check

1 driving 2 Drinking 3 studying 4 Selling
5 going

1 그의 직업은 버스를 운전하는 것이다.
2 물을 마시는 것은 당신의 건강에 좋다.
3 Mary는 영어 공부하는 것을 좋아한다.
4 장난감을 파는 것은 그의 직업이다.
5 그녀의 취미는 영화보러 가는 것이다.

Comprehension Check

1 a 2 a 3 b

1 남자의 직업은 꿀을 모으는 것이다.
2 벌집은 어디에 있는가?
3 무엇이 남자가 떨어지는 것을 막아주는가?

TRY IT

1) traditional 2) honey 3) cliffs
4) a rope ladder

꿀 모으기 관광
당신은 꿀 채집가가 될 수 있습니다.
그것은 네팔의 전통 직업입니다.
당신은 세계에서 가장 좋은 꿀을 얻을 수 있어요.
벌집은 절벽에 있기 때문에, 당신은 밧줄 사다리를 이용할 것입니다.
그것은 위험하지만 멋지답니다.

REVIEW TEST PP.100~101

1 hive 2 disappear 3 hold onto 4 doll
5 fall 6 pillow 7 worry 8 honey 9 cliff
10 take away 11 Playing soccer 12 collecting comic books 13 him my secrets[my secrets to him] 14 b 15 **a** True **b** False

1 hive: 벌집
2 disappear: 사라지다
3 hold onto: ~에 매달리다
4 doll: 인형
5 fall: 떨어지다
6 나는 잘 때 높은 베개를 사용한다.
7 영어 시험은 나에게 큰 걱정이다.
8 나는 주스에 꿀을 넣었다.
9 그 남자는 절벽을 기어오르고 있다.
10 이 약이 고통을 없애 줄 것이다.
11 축구를 하는 것은 재미있다.
12 내 취미는 만화책을 수집하는 것이다.
13 나는 그에게 내 비밀을 말해줄 것이다.
15 **a** 마야 인형은 슬퍼 보이지만 특별한 힘이 있다.
b 마야 인형은 사람들을 걱정하게 만든다.

MEMO

MEMO

MEMO

MEMO

지은이

NE능률 영어교육연구소

NE능률 영어교육연구소는 혁신적이며 효율적인 영어 교재를 개발하고
영어 학습의 질을 한 단계 높이고자 노력하는 NE능률의 연구조직입니다.

리딩버디 3

펴 낸 이	주민홍
펴 낸 곳	서울특별시 마포구 월드컵북로 396(상암동) 누리꿈스퀘어 비즈니스타워 10층 (주)NE능률 (우편번호 03925)
펴 낸 날	2016년 1월 5일 개정판 제1쇄 2023년 7월 15일 제14쇄
전 화	02 2014 7114
팩 스	02 3142 0356
홈페이지	www.neungyule.com
등록번호	제 1-68호
I S B N	979-11-253-0971-0 63740
정 가	10,000원

NE 능률

고객센터

교재 내용 문의 : contact.nebooks.co.kr (별도의 가입 절차 없이 작성 가능)
제품 구매, 교환, 불량, 반품 문의 : 02-2014-7114
☎ 전화문의는 본사 업무시간 중에만 가능합니다.

초등학생의 영어 친구

리딩버디

단어장

3

NE 능률

초등학생의 영어 친구

리딩버디

단어장

3

발음 기호를 배워봅시다.

하나의 알파벳이 여러 소리를 가지고 있는 경우가 있어서 같은 알파벳이라도 단어에 따라 소리가 달라집니다. 하지만 발음 기호를 알아두면 영어 단어를 정확하게 읽을 수 있답니다. 듣고 따라 하면서 발음 기호를 익혀봅시다.

★자음★

p	plate [pleit]
b	bad [bæd]
t	toy [tɔi]
d	did [did]
k	cozy [kóuzi]
g	get [get]
tʃ	chew [tʃuː]
dʒ	job [dʒɑb]
f	feed [fiːd]
v	visit [vízit]
θ	thing [θiŋ]
ð	they [ðei]
s	see [siː]
z	zoo [zuː]
ʃ	ship [ʃip]
ʒ	vision [víʒən]

h	have [həv]	l	leg [leg]
m	miss [mis]	r	run [rʌn]
n	note [nout]	j	yes [jes]
ŋ	sing [siŋ]	w	weak [wi:k]

☆ 모음 ☆

a	watch [wɑtʃ]	æ	cat [kæt]
e	pet [pet]	ʌ	peanut [pí:nʌ̀t]
i	wing [wiŋ]	ɔ	wall [wɔ:l]
o	grow [grou]	ə	pilot [páilət]
u	put [put]	ɛ	wear [wɛə*r*]

UNIT 01 MONEY

듣고 따라 말해 봅시다.

clerk [klə:rk] 점원

stone [stoun] 돌

plate [pleit] 접시

move [mu:v] 옮기다

thankfully [θǽŋkfəli] 고맙게도

carry [kǽri] 들고 다니다

remember [rimémbər]
기억하다

owner [óunər] 주인, 소유자

save [seiv] 저축하다

piggy bank [pígi bæ̀ŋk]
돼지 저금통

town [taun] 마을

piglet [píglit] 새끼 돼지

grow [grou] 자라다

sick [sik] 아픈

UNIT 02 ENVIRONMENT

듣고 따라 말해 봅시다.

mountain [máuntən] 산

climb [klaim] 오르다

heavy [hévi] 무거운

oxygen bottle
[ɑ́ksidʒən bɑ̀tl] 산소통

among [əmʌ́ŋ] ~ 중에서

hard [hɑːrd] 힘든

leave [liːv] ~을 그대로 두다

light [lait] 가벼운

trash [træʃ] 쓰레기

scientist [sáiəntist] 과학자

cow [kau] 소

hurt [həːrt] 다치게 하다
과거형 hurt

fart [fɑːrt] 방귀를 뀌다

burp [bəːrp] 트림하다

surprising [sərpráiziŋ] 놀라운

UNIT 03 MY OPINION

듣고 따라 말해 봅시다.

hallway [hɔ́ːlwèi] 복도

safe [seif] 안전한

enter [éntə*r*] 들어가다

behave [bihéiv] 행동하다

record [rikɔ́ː*r*d] 녹화하다

cf. record [rékə*r*d] 기록

uncomfortable
[ʌnkʌ́mfərtəbl] 불편한

place [pleis] 장소

study [stʌ́di] 공부하다

learn [ləːrn] 배우다

draw [drɔː] 그리다

outside [àutsáid] 밖에(서)

lake [leik] 호수

library [láibrèri] 도서관

nature [néitʃər] 자연

miss [mis] 그리워하다

UNIT 04 SHOPPING

듣고 따라 말해 봅시다.

cart [kɑːrt] 카트, 손수레

way [wei] 방법

reason [ríːzən] 이유

full [ful] 가득 찬

push [puʃ] 밀다

secret [síːkrit] 비밀

look for 찾다

flavor [fléivə*r*] 맛

price [prais] 가격

be made from
~로 만들어지다

farmer [fá:rmər] 농부

work [wə:rk] 일하다

cheaply [tʃí:pli] 싸게, 저렴하게

fair [fɛər] 공정한

UNIT 05 GOOD INVENTIONS

듣고 따라 말해 봅시다.

normal [nɔ́ːrməl] 평범한

ladder [lǽdər] 사다리

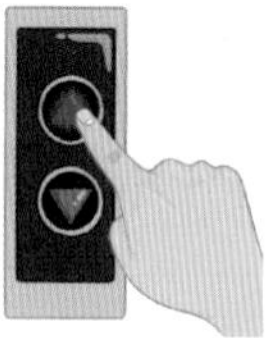

press [pres] 누르다

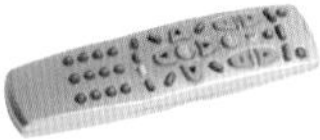

remote control
[rimóut kəntròul] 리모컨

pick up 집어 들다

technology [teknάlədʒi] 기술

convenient [kənvíːnjənt] 편리한

across [əkrɔ́ːs]
가로질러, 맞은편에

wait [weit] 기다리다

dangerous [déindʒərəs] 위험한

invent [invént] 발명하다

traffic light [trǽfik làit] 신호등

side [said] 쪽

dance [dæns] 춤을 추다

copy [kάpi] 따라 하다

UNIT 06 TECHNOLOGY

듣고 따라 말해 봅시다.

sign [sain] 표지판

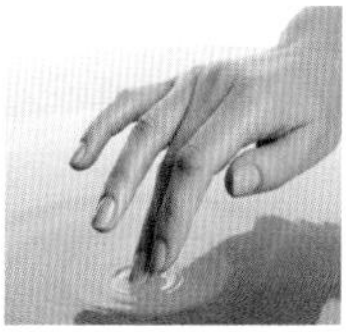

touch [tʌtʃ] 만지다

painting [péintiŋ] 그림

rule [ruːl] 규칙

visitor [vízitər] 방문객

blind [blaind] 시각 장애가 있는

restaurant [réstərənt]
식당, 레스토랑

ring [riŋ] 울리다

turn off (전원을) 끄다

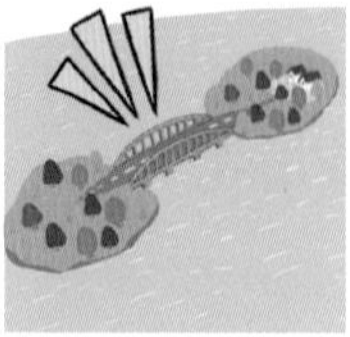

connect [kənékt] 연결하다

machine [məʃíːn] 기계

together [təgéðər] 함께

control [kəntróul] 조종하다

break down 고장 나다

UNIT 07 IN SPACE

듣고 따라 말해 봅시다.

astronaut [ǽstrənɔ̀ːt]
우주비행사

space [speis] 우주

float [flout] (공중에서) 떠가다

spaceship [spéisʃìp] 우주선

tie [tai] 묶다

toilet [tɔ́ilit] 변기

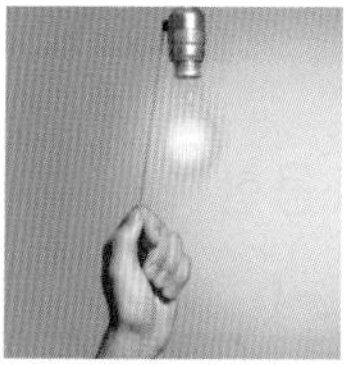

turn on (전기 등을) 켜다

listen [lísn] 듣다

shoot [ʃuːt] (총 등을) 쏘다

loud [laud] 시끄러운

real [rí:əl] 진짜의

silent [sáilənt] 조용한

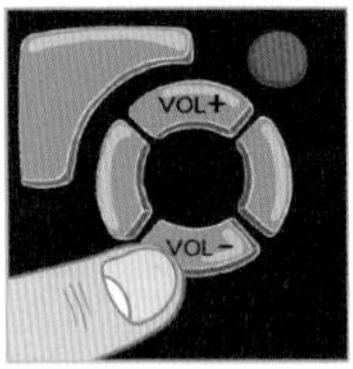

turn down (소리 등을) 낮추다

volume [válju:m] 소리

UNIT 08 TRADITIONS

듣고 따라 말해 봅시다.

doll [dɑl] 인형

sad [sæd] 슬픈

worry [wə́ːri] 걱정

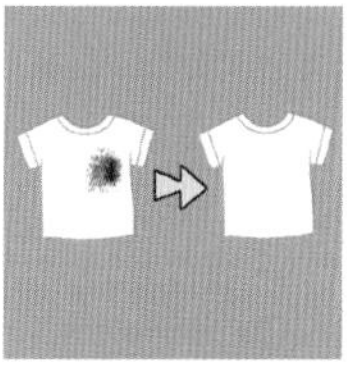

take away 없애 주다

pillow [pílou] 베개

disappear [dìsəpíər] 사라지다

rope [roup] 밧줄

hang from
~에서 매달리다, ~에서 드리워지다

cliff [klif] 절벽

hold onto ~에 매달리다

honey [hʌ́ni] 꿀

stick [stik] 막대

hive [haiv] 벌집

fall [fɔːl] 떨어지다

MEMO

MEMO

MEMO

MEMO

MEMO

NE능률 교재 MAP

독해

아래 교재 MAP을 참고하여 본인의 현재 혹은 목표 수준에 따라 교재를 선택하세요.
NE능률 교재들과 함께 영어실력을 쑥쑥~ 올려보세요!
MP3 등 교재 부가 학습 서비스 및 자세한 교재 정보는 www.nebooks.co.kr 에서 확인하세요.

초1-2
- 초등영어 리딩이 된다 Start 1
- 초등영어 리딩이 된다 Start 2
- 초등영어 리딩이 된다 Start 3
- 초등영어 리딩이 된다 Start 4

초3
- 리딩버디 1

초3-4
- 리딩버디 2
- 초등영어 리딩이 된다 Basic 1
- 초등영어 리딩이 된다 Basic 2
- 초등영어 리딩이 된다 Basic 3
- 초등영어 리딩이 된다 Basic 4

초4-5
- 리딩버디 3
- 주니어 리딩튜터 스타터 1

초5-6
- 초등영어 리딩이 된다 Jump 1
- 초등영어 리딩이 된다 Jump 2
- 초등영어 리딩이 된다 Jump 3
- 초등영어 리딩이 된다 Jump 4
- 주니어 리딩튜터 스타터 2

초6-예비중
- 1316팬클럽 독해 1
- 주니어 리딩튜터 1
- Junior Reading Expert 1
- Reading Forward Basic 1

중1
- 주니어 리딩튜터 2
- Junior Reading Expert 2
- Reading Forward Basic 2
- 열중 16강 독해+문법 1
- Reading Inside Starter

중1-2
- 1316팬클럽 독해 2
- 주니어 리딩튜터 3
- 정말 기특한 구문독해 입문
- Junior Reading Expert 3
- Reading Forward Intermediate 1
- 열중 16강 독해+문법 2
- Reading Inside 1

중2-3
- 1316팬클럽 독해 3
- 주니어 리딩튜터 4
- 정말 기특한 구문독해 기본
- Junior Reading Expert 4
- Reading Forward Intermediate 2
- Reading Inside 2

중3
- 리딩튜터 입문
- 정말 기특한 구문독해 완성
- Reading Forward Advanced 1
- 열중 16강 독해+문법 3
- Reading Inside 3

중3-예비고
- Reading Expert 1
- 리딩튜터 기본
- Reading Forward Advanced 2

고1
- 빠바 기초세우기
- 리딩튜터 실력
- Reading Expert 2
- TEPS BY STEP G+R Basic

고1-2
- 빠바 구문독해
- 리딩튜터 수능 PLUS
- Reading Expert 3

고2-3, 수능 실전
- 빠바 유형독해
- 빠바 종합실전편
- Reading Expert 4
- TEPS BY STEP G+R 1

고3 이상, 수능 고난도
- Reading Expert 5
- 능률 고급영문독해

수능 이상/ 토플 80-89 · 텝스 600-699점
- ADVANCED Reading Expert 1
- TEPS BY STEP G+R 2
- RADIX TOEFL Blue Label Reading 1,2

수능 이상/ 토플 90-99 · 텝스 700-799점
- ADVANCED Reading Expert 2
- RADIX TOEFL Black Label Reading 1

수능 이상/ 토플 100 · 텝스 800점 이상
- RADIX TOEFL Black Label Reading 2
- TEPS BY STEP G+R 3

초등학생의 영어 친구

리딩버디

WORKBOOK

3

NE 능률

초등학생의 영어 친구

리딩버디

WORKBOOK

3

UNIT 01 ☆ MONEY STORY 01

[1~3] Look at the pictures and choose the correct word.

thankfully	owner	carry

1 

____

2 

____

3 

____

[4~5] Choose the right word for the blanks.

stones	clerk

4 당신은 점원에게 돈을 준다.

→ You give money to the ____________.

5 야프 섬에서는 물건을 사기 위해 돌들을 사용한다.

→ People use ____________ to buy things on Yap Island.

[6~8] Read and write in the correct order.

6 Jason은 Kevin만큼 나이가 들었다.

Jason / is / old / Kevin / as / as

→ ______________________________

7 작은 돌들은 정찬용 접시만큼 작다.

dinner plates / small stones / small / as / are / as

→ ______________________________

8 이 돌은 나만큼 크다.

me / as / this stone / is / as / big

→ ______________________________

[9~11] Read and complete the sentences.

9 큰 돌들은 키 큰 남자 두 명만큼 크다.

→ Big stones ______________________ two tall men.

10 그 접시는 내 손만큼 작다.

→ The plate ______________________ my hand.

11 그 나무는 집만큼 높다.

→ The tree ______________________ the house.

[1~2] Look at the pictures and write the words correctly three times.

1  **asev** ____________ ____________ ____________

2  **ksci** ____________ ____________ ____________

[3~5] Choose the right words for the blanks.

grew	piggy banks	piglet

3 왜 사람들은 돼지 저금통에 돈을 저금하는가?

→ Why do people save money in ____________?

4 Wilbur는 새끼 돼지를 샀다.

→ Wilbur bought a ____________.

5 그 돼지는 점점 더 자랐다.

→ The pig ____________ and ____________.

[6~8] Read and write in the correct order.

6 그 새끼 돼지는 새끼 고양이보다 더 크다.

the kitten / bigger / the piglet / is / than

→ ______________________________

7 Tom은 Jake보다 키가 더 크다.

Jake / Tom / taller / is / than

→ ______________________________

8 과학은 영어보다 더 쉽다.

easier/ English / than / science / is

→ ______________________________

[9~11] Read and complete the sentences.

9 그 새끼 돼지는 Wilbur보다 훨씬 더 작았다.

→ The piglet was much ____________________ Wilbur.

10 그 강아지는 닭보다 더 작다.

→ The puppy ____________________.

11 그 돼지는 Wilbur보다 더 커졌다.

→ The pig became ____________________.

[1~2] Look at the pictures and choose the correct word.

light	heavy

1 

____

2 

____

[3~5] Choose the right word for the blanks.

climb	among	trash

3 산소통은 그것들 중에서 가장 무거운 것이다.

→ Oxygen bottles are the heaviest things __________ them.

4 많은 사람들은 에베레스트 산을 오르려고 노력한다.

→ Many people try to __________ Mt. Everest.

5 등산객들은 그들의 쓰레기를 에베레스트 산에 두고 온다.

→ The climbers leave their __________ on Mt. Everest.

[6~8] Read and write in the correct order.

6 대구는 세 곳 중 가장 더운 도시이다.

of the three / the hottest city / Daegu / is

→ ______________________________

7 초록색 가방은 세 개 중에 가장 비싼 가방이다.

is / the green bag / the most expensive bag / of the three

→ ______________________________

8 Bill은 그의 반에서 가장 키가 큰 학생이다.

Bill / in his class / the tallest student / is

→ ______________________________

[9~11] Read and complete the sentences.

9 에베레스트 산은 세계에서 가장 높은 산이다.

→ Mt. Everest is ______________________________.

10 Alex는 세 명 중 가장 무거운 소년이다.

→ Alex ______________________________.

11 Halla는 세 개 중에 가장 낮은 빌딩이다.

→ Halla ______________________________.

[1~3] Look at the pictures and write the words correctly three times.

1  **rfat** __________ __________ __________

2  **urth** __________ __________ __________

3  **prbu** __________ __________ __________

[4~5] Choose the right word for the blanks.

cows	scientists

4 과학자들은 소들이 지구를 해친다고 말한다.

→ __________ say that cows are hurting the Earth.

5 소들이 내뿜는 가스는 공기를 아주 뜨겁게 만들고 있다.

→ The gas from __________ is making the air too hot.

[6~8] Read and write in the correct order.

6 이 뉴스는 정말 재미있구나!

this news / how/ is / funny

→ ______________________________

7 그것은 정말 귀여운 고양이이구나!

a / it / what / cat / is/ cute/

→ ______________________________

8 그 게임은 정말 흥미롭구나!

exciting / how / is / the game

→ ______________________________

[9~11] Read and complete the sentences.

9 바닥이 정말 더럽구나! (how)

→ ______________________________ is!

10 정말 아름다운 그림들이구나! (what)

→ ______________________________

11 정말 놀라운 뉴스이구나! (what)

→ ______________________________

[1~2] Look at the pictures and write the words correctly three times.

1  **dcrore** ____________ ____________ ____________

2  **ywlhala** ____________ ____________ ____________

[3~5] Choose the right word for the blanks.

behave	enter	uncomfortable

3 학생들은 불편하다고 느낀다.

→ Students feel ____________.

4 나쁜 사람들은 학교에 들어올 수 없다.

→ Bad people can't ____________ the school.

5 학생들은 나쁘게 행동하지 않을 것이다.

→ Students will not ____________ badly.

[6~8] Read and write in the correct order.

6 그 비누는 좋은 냄새가 난다.

the soap / good / smells

→ ______________________________

7 그 새 의자는 편안해 보인다.

looks /comfortable / the new chair

→ ______________________________

8 그 음악은 슬프게 들렸다.

sad / the music / sounded

→ ______________________________

[9~11] Read and complete the sentences.

9 학생들은 학교에서 안전하다고 느낄 수 있다.

→ Students can ____________________ in school.

10 그 피자는 맛있다.

→ The pizza ____________________.

11 그 아이디어는 재미있게 들린다.

→ ______________________________

[1 ~ 3] Look at the pictures and choose the correct word.

outside	miss	nature

1 

____

2 

____

3 

____

[4 ~ 6] Choose the right word for the blanks.

lakes	learn	draw

4 나는 항상 집과 다른 장소에서 배운다.

→ I always ____________ at home and other places.

5 John은 밖에서 그림 그리는 것을 좋아한다.

→ John likes to ____________ outside.

6 그의 부모님은 호수에 그를 자주 데려가신다.

→ His parents often take him to ____________.

[7~9] Read and write in the correct order.

7 그는 때때로 그의 친구들이 그립다.

his friends / sometimes / misses

→ He ______________________________.

8 John은 절대 학교에 가지 않는다.

never / school / goes / to

→ John ______________________________.

9 나는 항상 늦게 일어난다.

wake up / late / always

→ I ______________________________.

[10~12] Read and complete the sentences.

10 Ron은 때때로 아침을 먹는다.

→ Ron ______________________________ breakfast.

11 지난 주에 비가 자주 내렸다.

→ Last week, ______________________________.

12 학생들은 보통 학교에서 공부한다.

→ Students ______________________________.

[1~2] Look at the pictures and write the words correctly three times.

1  **trca** ______ ______ ______

2  **lulf** ______ ______ ______

[3~6] Choose the right word for the blanks.

secret	push	reasons	way

3 쇼핑몰은 특별한 이유들로 카트들을 크게 만든다.

→ Malls make carts big for special ______.

4 쇼핑 카트가 이렇게 하는 것의 한 방법이다.

→ Carts are one ______ of doing this.

5 크고 무거운 카트는 쇼핑몰의 큰 비밀이다.

→ Big and heavy carts are the big ______ for malls.

6 사람들은 무거운 카트를 빠르게 밀 수 없다.

→ People can't ______ heavy carts fast.

[7~9] Read and write in the correct order.

7 그 책은 그를 유명하게 만들었다.

him / made / the book / famous

→ ______________________________

8 쇼핑몰은 사람들이 더 많은 것을 사게 만들기 위해 노력한다.

malls / people / buy more things / try to make

→ ______________________________

9 나의 선생님은 우리가 많은 숙제를 하게 만들었다.

us / made / do a lot of homework / my teacher

→ ______________________________

[10~12] Read and complete the sentences.

10 그 음악은 나를 슬프게 만들었다.

→ The music ______________________.

11 Jim은 사람들을 웃게 만든다.

→ Jim always ______________________.

12 이 소스는 어떤 음식이라도 맛있게 만들 수 있다.

→ This sauce can ______________________.

[1~3] Look at the pictures and choose the correct word.

price	look for	be made from

1 

____

2 

____

3 

____

[4~6] Choose the right word for the blanks.

flavor	fair	cheaply

4 몇몇 사람들은 이것이 공정하지 않다고 생각한다.

→ Some people think this is not ____________.

5 내가 가장 좋아하는 아이스크림 맛은 초콜릿이다.

→ My favorite ____________ of ice cream is chocolate.

6 대기업들은 카카오 열매를 너무 싸게 산다.

→ Big companies buy cocoa beans too ____________.

[7~9] Read and write in the correct order.

7 나는 어렸을 때 미국에서 살았다.

a child / I / when / was

→ I lived in the USA ______________________.

8 어젯밤 Tom은 아팠기 때문에 일찍 잠자리에 들었다.

because / sick / Tom / was

→ Last night, ______________________, he went to bed early.

9 내가 민수를 만난다면 나는 매우 기쁠 것이다.

I / if / Minsu / meet

→ ______________________, I will be very happy.

[10~12] Read and complete the sentences.

10 내가 내일 시험이 있기 때문에, 공부를 해야 한다.

→ ______________________, I have to study.

11 당신은 생선을 살 때, 그것들의 눈 색깔을 확인해라.

→ ______________________, check the color of their eyes.

12 만약 그 창문이 열려 있다면, 그것을 닫아라.

→ ______________________, close it.

UNIT 05 ☆ GOOD INVENTIONS STORY 01

[1~3] Look at the pictures and choose the correct word.

remote control	technology	press

1 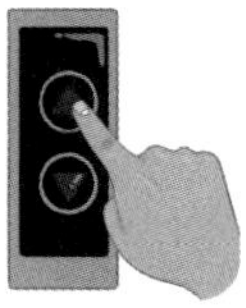

____

2 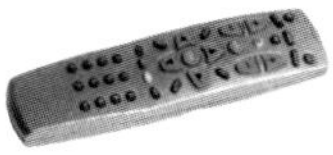

____

3 

____

[4~6] Choose the right words for the blanks.

convenient	pick up	normal

4 그것은 평범해 보이지만 다르다.

→ It looks __________, but it is different.

5 드론들이 신발을 집으러 날아간다.

→ The drones fly to __________ the shoes.

6 기술이 쇼핑을 더욱 편리하게 만든다.

→ Technology makes shopping more __________.

[7~9] Read and write in the correct order.

7 그 차는 맛이 좋다.

tastes / the tea / good

→ ______________________________

8 그 로봇들은 사람 같아 보인다.

like / men / the robots / look

→ ______________________________

9 그 신발은 편안해 보인다.

comfortable / look / the shoes

→ ______________________________

[10~12] Read and complete the sentences.

10 그 수프는 카레 같은 맛이 난다.

→ The soup ____________________ curry.

11 그것들은 비행기처럼 보인다.

→ They ____________________ airplanes.

12 그 초는 장미 같은 냄새가 난다.

→ The candle ____________________ roses.

[1~3] Look at the pictures and write the words correctly three times.

1  ypco ______ ______ ______

2  deis ______ ______ ______

3  netvni ______ ______ ______

[4~5] Choose the right words for the blanks.

across	traffic light

4 사람들은 춤추는 신호등을 보는 것을 즐긴다.

→ People enjoy watching the dancing ______.

5 어떤 사람들은 빨간불에 길을 건넌다.

→ Some people walk ______ the road at red lights.

[6~8] Read and write in the correct order.

6 나는 그것에 대해 알고 싶다.

to / know about it / I / want

→ ____________________

7 현아는 책 읽기를 끝냈다.

reading / the book / Hyuna / finished

→ ____________________

8 그들은 기다리는 것을 즐긴다.

waiting / enjoy / they

→ ____________________

[9~11] Read and complete the sentences.

9 Jake는 사람들 앞에서 춤추는 것을 즐긴다.

→ Jake ____________________ in front of people.

10 그들은 그들의 숙제를 먼저 하기로 결정했다.

→ They ____________________ first.

11 그는 아이스크림을 먹고 싶어한다.

→ He ____________________.

[1~3] Look at the pictures and write the words correctly three times.

1  **tanpinig** ______________ ______________ ______________

2  **leru** ______________ ______________ ______________

3  **ngsi** ______________ ______________ ______________

[4~5] Choose the right word for the blanks.

visitors	blind

4 이것은 시각 장애인들에게 좋은 소식이다.

→ This is good news for ____________ people.

5 방문객들은 그림들을 만져도 된다.

→ ____________ may touch the paintings.

[6~8] Read and write in the correct order.

6 그녀는 이 액션 영화를 좋아할지도 모른다.

may / like / she / this action movie

→ ______________________________

7 이 그림 만져도 되나요?

touch / this picture / I / may

→ ______________________________

8 당신은 내 스마트폰을 사용해도 된다.

you / use / my smartphone / may

→ ______________________________

[9~11] Read and complete the sentences.

9 당신은 미술관에서 이 표시를 볼지도 모른다.

→ You ____________________ this sign in art museums.

10 당신은 여기서 사진을 찍으면 안 된다.

→ You ____________________ pictures here.

11 그 그림들은 그다지 깨끗하지 않을지도 모른다.

→ The paintings ____________________ so clean.

[1~2] Look at the pictures and choose the correct word.

machine	connect

1 

____

2 

____

[3~5] Choose the right words for the blanks.

break down	control	turn off

3 당신은 당신의 스마트폰으로 물건들을 조종할 수 있다.

→ You can ______________ things with your smartphone.

4 그녀는 자신의 전화기를 사용해서 난방을 끈다.

→ She uses her phone to ______________ her heating.

5 바이러스가 공격하면, 모든 기계가 고장 날 것이다.

→ If a virus attacks, all machines will ______________.

[6~8] Read and write in the correct order.

6 나는 통화중이다.

talking / am / on the phone / I

→ ______________________________

7 우리 아버지는 빨간 자동차를 운전하고 있다.

driving / a red car / my father / is

→ ______________________________

8 그들은 중국어를 공부하고 있다.

they / Chinese / are / studying

→ ______________________________

[9~11] Read and complete the sentences.

9 인터넷이 기계들을 함께 연결하고 있다.

→ The Internet ______________ machines together.

10 Jenny는 음식점에서 먹고 있다.

→ Jenny ______________ at a restaurant.

11 소라는 컴퓨터 게임을 하고 있다.

→ Sora ______________ computer games.

[1~2] Look at the pictures and choose the correct word.

spaceship	tie

1 

____

2 

____

[3~5] Choose the right word for the blanks.

astronaut	space	float

3 그녀는 우주를 여행한다.

→ She travels into __________.

4 Jane은 우주비행사이다.

→ Jane is a(n) __________.

5 그녀의 음식은 우주선을 떠다닐 수 있다.

→ Her food can __________ around in the spaceship.

[6~8] Read and write in the correct order.

6 그는 횡단보도에서 조심해야 한다.

be careful / he / at the crosswalk / must

→ ______________________________

7 도서관 안에서는 조용히 해야 한다.

have to / you / in the library / be quiet

→ ______________________________

8 그녀는 화장실의 변기에 자신을 묶어야만 한다.

tie herself / she / to the toilet / must

→ ______________________________

[9~11] Read and complete the sentences.

9 그녀가 먹을 때, 그녀는 조심해야만 한다.

→ When she eats, ______________________________.

10 그녀가 잘 때, 그녀는 자신을 침대에 묶어야만 한다.

→ When she sleeps, ______________________________ to the bed.

11 나는 헬멧을 써야 한다.

→ ______________________________ a helmet.

[1~3] Look at the pictures and write the words correctly three times.

1  **uodl** ______ ______ ______

2  **entlis** ______ ______ ______

3  **ostoh** ______ ______ ______

[4~5] Choose the right words for the blanks.

turn on	turn down

4 TV를 켜라.

→ ______ the TV.

5 다음 번에 〈스타워즈〉를 볼 때는, 볼륨을 낮춰라!

→ Next time you watch *Star Wars*, ______ the volume!

[6~8] Read and write in the correct order.

6 그는 아픈 것이 틀림 없다.

sick / must / he / be

→ ______________________________

7 그 이야기는 사실일 리가 없다.

cannot / be / the story / true

→ ______________________________

8 Star Wars는 매우 재미있음이 틀림 없다.

Star Wars / very exciting / be / must

→ ______________________________

[9~11] Read the complete the sentences.

9 이 소리들은 진짜일 리가 없다!

→ These sounds ____________________ real!

10 그 영화는 틀린 것이 틀림없다.

→ The movie ____________________ wrong.

11 그들은 자고 있다. 그들이 컴퓨터를 사용할 리가 없다.

→ They are sleeping. They ____________________ the computer.

UNIT 08 ☆ TRADITIONS STORY 01

[1~3] Look at the pictures and choose the correct word.

doll	pillow	worry

1 

____

2 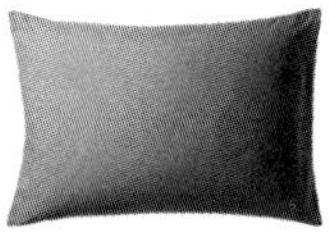

____

3 

____

[4~5] Choose the right words for the blanks.

takes away	disappear

4 그녀는 아침쯤에 그녀의 걱정이 사라지기를 바란다.

→ She hopes her worries __________ by the morning.

5 그 인형은 Lucy의 걱정을 없애 준다.

→ The doll __________ Lucy's worries.

[6~8] Read and write in the correct order.

6 우리 오빠는 나에게 그의 비밀을 말해줬다.

my brother / to me / told / his secret

→ ______________________________

7 우리 선생님은 우리에게 그 소식을 말해주었다.

told / the news / us / my teacher

→ ______________________________

8 내 이야기를 너에게 말해줄게.

I / my story / will tell / to you

→ ______________________________

[9~11] Read and complete the sentences.

9 Lucy는 그녀의 걱정들을 자신의 인형에게 말했다.

→ Lucy ______________________ to her doll.

10 나는 그에게 내 비밀을 말해줄 것이다.

→ I will ______________________.

11 마야인들은 인형들에게 그들의 걱정들을 말했다.

→ Mayan people ______________________.

[1~3] Look at the pictures and write the words correctly three times.

1  **iflfc** ____________ ____________ ____________

2  **enohy** ____________ ____________ ____________

3  **vehi** ____________ ____________ ____________

[4~5] Choose the right words for the blanks.

hangs from	falling

4 긴 밧줄 사다리가 절벽 꼭대기에서부터 드리워져 있다.

→ A long rope ladder ______________ the top of a cliff.

5 사다리만이 그가 떨어지는 것을 방지할 수 있다.

→ Only the ladder can keep him from ______________.

[6~8] Read and write in the correct order.

6 Mary는 영어 공부를 좋아한다.

Mary / English / studying / likes

→ ______________________________

7 그의 직업은 버스를 운전하는 것이다.

driving / his job / a bus / is

→ ______________________________

8 장난감을 파는 것은 그의 직업이다.

toys / selling / his job / is

→ ______________________________

[9~11] Read and complete the sentences.

9 그녀의 취미는 영화보러 가는 것이다.

→ Her hobby is ______________________.

10 그의 직업은 꿀을 모으는 것이다.

→ His job is ______________________.

11 물을 마시는 것은 당신의 건강에 좋다.

→ ______________________ good for your health.

★ 정답 ★

UNIT 01 ☆ MONEY

STORY 01 PP.2~3

1 owner 2 carry 3 thankfully 4 clerk 5 stones 6 Jason is as old as Kevin. 7 Small stones are as small as dinner plates. 8 This stone is as big as me. 9 are as big as 10 is as small as 11 is as tall[high] as

STORY 02 PP.4~5

1 save 2 sick 3 piggy banks 4 piglet 5 grew 6 The piglet is bigger than the kitten. 7 Tom is taller than Jake. 8 Science is easier than English. 9 smaller than 10 is smaller than the chicken 11 bigger than Wilbur

UNIT 02 ☆ ENVIRONMENT

STORY 01 PP.6~7

1 heavy 2 light 3 among 4 climb 5 trash 6 Daegu is the hottest city of the three. 7 The green bag is the most expensive bag of the three. 8 Bill is the tallest student in his class. 9 the highest mountain in the world 10 is the heaviest boy of the three 11 is the lowest building of the three

STORY 02 PP.8~9

1 fart 2 hurt 3 burp 4 Scientists 5 cows 6 How funny this news is! 7 What a cute cat it is! 8 How exciting the game is! 9 How dirty the floor 10 What beautiful pictures[paintings]! 11 What surprising news!

UNIT 03 ☆ MY OPINION

STORY 01 PP.10~11

1 record 2 hallway 3 uncomfortable 4 enter 5 behave 6 The soap smells good. 7 The new chair looks comfortable. 8 The music sounded sad. 9 feel safe 11 tastes delicious 12 The idea sounds interesting.

STORY 02 PP.12~13

1 nature 2 outside 3 miss 4 learn 5 draw 6 lakes 7 sometimes misses his friends 8 never goes to school 9 always wake up late 10 sometimes eats 11 it often rained 12 usually study at school

UNIT 04 ☆ SHOPPING

STORY 01 PP.14~15

1 cart 2 full 3 reasons 4 way 5 secret 6 push 7 The book made him famous. 8 Malls try to make people buy more things. 9 My teacher made us do a lot of homework. 10 made me sad 11 makes people laugh 12 make any food delicious

STORY 02 PP.16~17

1 look for 2 price 3 be made from 4 fair 5 flavor 6 cheaply 7 when I was a child 8 because Tom was sick 9 If I meet Minsu 10 Because I have a test tomorrow 11 When you buy fish 12 If the window is open

UNIT 05 ★ GOOD INVENTIONS

STORY 01 PP.18~19

1 press 2 remote control 3 technology 4 normal 5 pick up 6 convenient 7 The tea tastes good. 8 The robots look like men. 9 The shoes look comfortable. 10 tastes like 11 look like 12 smells like

STORY 02 PP.20~21

1 copy 2 side 3 invent 4 traffic light 5 across 6 I want to know about it. 7 Hyuna finished reading the book. 8 They enjoy waiting. 9 enjoys dancing 10 decided to do their homework 11 wants to eat ice cream

UNIT 06 ★ TECHNOLOGY

STORY 01 PP.22~23

1 painting 2 rule 3 sign 4 blind 5 Visitors 6 She may like this action movie. 7 May I touch this picture? 8 You may use my smartphone. 9 may see 10 may not take 11 may not be

STORY 02 PP.24~25

1 connect 2 machine 3 control 4 turn off 5 break down 6 I am talking on the phone. 7 My father is driving a red car. 8 They are studying Chinese. 9 is connecting 10 is eating 11 is playing

UNIT 07 ★ IN SPACE

STORY 01 PP.26~27

1 tie 2 spaceship 3 space 4 astronaut 5 float 6 He must be careful at the crosswalk. 7 You have to be quiet in the library. 8 She must tie herself to the toilet. 9 she must[has to] be careful 10 she must[has to] tie herself 11 I have to[must] wear

STORY 02 PP.28~29

1 loud 2 silent 3 shoot 4 Turn on 5 turn down 6 He must be sick. 7 The story cannot be true. 8 Star Wars must be very exciting. 9 cannot be 10 must be 11 cannot use

UNIT 08 ★ TRADITIONS

STORY 01 PP.30~31

1 worry 2 pillow 3 doll 4 disappear 5 takes away 6 My bother told his secret to me. 7 My teacher told us the news. 8 I will tell my story to you. 9 told her worries 10 tell him my secret[tell my secret to him] 11 told dolls their worries[told their worries to dolls]

STORY 02 PP.32~33

1 cliff 2 honey 3 hive 4 hangs from 5 falling 6 Mary likes studying English. 7 His job is driving a bus. 8 Selling toys is his job. 9 going to the movies 10 collecting honey 11 Drinking water is

MEMO

MEMO

MEMO

MEMO

MEMO